THE

MYSTERIES AND MISERIES

OF

New York:

A STORY OF REAL LIFE,

BY NED BUNTLINE.

~~~~~~~~

PART II.

NEW YORK:

EDWARD Z. C. JUDSON.

1848.

PREFATORIAL TO THE SECOND PART.

THE unexampled and heart-cheering success of the first part of this work has given its author a hope that in the second, he will not fail to be equally pleasing to the readers of the first.

He has now the satisfaction of knowing that his labors are appreciated not only by the good, but by the very villains whom he had *commenced to* ash; for the first have cheered him by an unexpected and unparalled patronage; the second have shown by their threats, anonymous letters c., that they *feel* the *truth* which he has uttered.

And one word of consolation to these last. The writer is one who can neither be bribed from his duty, or frightened from his course. He depends upon that Being for protection, who has before-time saved him from the assassin's hand; and whose power has upheld him in perils which he cares not now to allude to, but which were incurred in performing a *duty* like that in which he is now engaged. To those who may have thought that fair words and bright promises might deter us from throwing our Drummond light on their dark deeds we can only say—you are mistaken in our character. We cannot be bought.

To those who have threatened us—we have no reply, save that we are ever on the look-out for them, and are not at all principled against destroying snakes or mad-dogs, when they attempt to bite us. We have commenced *gently* with the gamblers and thieves—the future pages will show wether their threats will make us touch them less lightly.

One word to some of our discerning and talented city critics. Some of you in your kind reviews of my first number have expressed an opinion that some of its scenes are over-wrought and untrue. This is not so. I pledge myself, if you will take the trouble to go with me, to show you an original, or counterpart for every scene which I have described.

N. B.

PART SECOND.

CHAPTER I.

THERE were many sad, and very few bright scenes in our last volume; we will endeavor to commence this less gloomily. Fancy is a kind creature, reader; an angel of the mind, which often ministers sunshine when the clouds of reality are around us.

Let her take you to a house on the Third avenue, where every sign of wealth and elegance is visible, externally and internally. You may have seen some of the up-town palaces of our merchant-kings, *kings* we say, because wealth makes power here; if so, I need not trouble you with the description, or myself with writing it.

In her chamber sat a mother—a sweet, lovely creature was she—her age could not be over twenty, and yet a bright-eyed child of at least four summers' blossoming, sat in her lap. Her eyes were dark blue, and that boy looked up at her with eyes blue as the shadowed ocean, and liquid too with affection were they, as is the bedewed violet's cup, when its slender stem is bent at the early dawn to greet the sun-rise. His chubby little face was set in a frame of golden curls, and she twined her fair fingers amid the silken tresses, and gazed down upon him with a fond pride—only to be felt by a young, happy mother, who looks upon her idolized first-born.

The child was playing with one of her soft brown ringlets that dropped within his reach, escaping from a cluster which lay thick upon her snowy shoulders, and prattling in that sweet broken tongue which none but infants learning first to imitate their parents' words can speak.

The door of the chamber opened and a young man, perchance of twenty-six or eight years, entered. He was about the middle height, well formed, and wore the unmistakeable look of a. gentleman. A glance at his light brown hair and clear blue eyes at once showed the relation which he held to the cherub we have described.

"*Dear* Annie!" said the gentleman as he entered, and with a hasty step he crossed the carpet and folding his arms around her and his boy, kissed his young wife tenderly.

And she—the beautiful mother looked up and kissed his fair high brow and murmured:—"My *own* dear Edward!" in tones that spoke her fondness. They were the deep-voiced echoes of a full, true heart.

And the little cherub too raised his pouting mouth and lisped—Give Willie a kiss too, Papa!"

"Yes, my boy, yes!" and while the father raised his child in his arms he said to her who bore it—

"Oh my Annie, you have made me but too, *too* happy. I often fear that we who are now so blessed will yet feel the touch of sorrow, for in life as with the elements—it cannot always be sunlight. The storm may, the night *must* come."

"But, dearest, should it, are we not together? You have borne prosperity well, you have a firmness and energy that will never fail you when misfortune comes. It is easier for a true man to bear adversity, than for a bad one to bear prosperity. To some, misfortune is necessary; as with the grape, they must be crushed ere the true essence of the character, the strong spirit of the *man* is expressed."

"Yes, Annie—I could breast the storm, but for you, for our child should I tremble."

"Are we not so linked together, Edward, that each to the other will be a support--even as the thick growing trees of the forest aid each other to withstand the blast?"

"True, dear one, we are linked together—yet as is the oak to the vine which clings around it, am I to you; as the budding rose which starts from the sod beneath, is our child to us both. The bud may easily be crushed, the vine may be torn from the oak, and yet the strong tree survive them both."

The large eyes of the young wife filled with tears. "Let us not talk so sadly," she murmured, "let us not paint for ourselves a clouded sky—but wait till it comes."

"We will change the subject," replied he—"but yet it is best sometimes to think of that which may be, for then we will be the better prepared for it, when it comes."

"True, dear one, but I will sing you a song now and that will remind us of the past, which is even as dear to us as the present. I will sing you your *own*—the one you used to sing to me when we were first wedded."

Leaving the boy in his father's arms, the young wife passed across the room and taking up a guitar which stood carelessly in a corner, returned to her seat, tuned it and sung in a low, deep voice, which seemed to fill the room with soulful melody—

THE SONG OF THE HEART.

I.

A pure heart and a peaceful mind
　And a soul above despair,
Which upward looks and leaves behind
　The heavy clouds of care;
And a dear wife smiling nigh
　With her baby by her side :
O, that is the life I'd choose,
　Of all the world beside.

II.

O, for a life that's wild and free,
　A thoughtless one may cry ;
But give a life of peace to me,
　A clear and cloudless sky,
And a loved one smiling nigh,
　My comfort and my pride,
O, that is the life I'd choose
　Of all the world beside.

III.

There are tempests loud and high
　And sorrows ever near,
But the star of hope is in the sky
　To light our pathway here,
Then we'll let the tempests blow
　And let the troubles come,
The lamp of love will brightly glow
　With light where'er we roam.

She ceased, and yet it seemed as if the echoes of her voice dwelt still in the room, even as if they *could* not die, for her

smiles, her looks of love were still the same—and these were re-
flected in the face of her husband and his boy.

Oh, why should ever a cloud come over their joy? And how
could it? Edward Abingdon was rich, respected by all who
knew him, beloved by a devoted wife. His fortune was not in-
vested in stocks, or in those gambling schemes and lotteries of
speculation which are as uncertain as the caprices of a coquette;
therefore poverty could not well approach him. He had not even
trusted to a "Bank," which, with such fate as *has been*, might
break, or be robbed by its officers, or the more honorable burglar.
He had fifty thousand dollars in cash there in that house; he
owned a block of buildings—the very block of which his dwelling made one. These, with their rent, gave him a princely in-
come on which to live and to entertain his cherished friends.

But we will now leave him and his, to turn to other scenes
which must be woven in our web.

The first which we shall present is this.

Harry Whitmore sat by the side of Isabella Meadows. Her
down-cast look—her blushing cheeks told not that he was saying
aught improper to her. Had his intentions been pure and honorable he was not speaking one word that she should blush for—
yet he, the heartless villain was breathing vows to her which he
neither intended to fulfil or even felt—he was telling her that she
had won the first pure love of his heart, praying her not only to
give him her affection but her hand.

She blushed; for this was the first time that her ears had ever
listened to words like these; never before had her heart known

that gush of sympathy which is felt by that which knows it is beloved.

His words were not displeasing to her, for she who had seen so little of the ways of the world was indeed struck with his fine *personalle*, his plausible and agreeable manners, and his apparent devotion to her. He was so fond of her brother too that she could scarcely help loving him. Therefore, though her eyes were downcast and her head slightly turned away, Harry knew that in winning her love, at least, his success was certain. He saw that in either eye a tear glittered beneath the drooping lashes, he noticed that her red lips quivered and her bosom heaved, though she did not speak. But he was not satisfied with this proof of her feelings. Again he repeated his last declaration:

"Dear Isabella, I have laid open my very heart to you; I have told you that your goodness more than your beauty has won from me a love as pure as it is fervent. Will you not reply—will you not bid me hope for a return?"

"Oh, Harry—*dear* Harry! how can I speak?" murmured the fair girl—and tears, great bright tears, rushed down her cheeks, as the dew from the full blown rose when its stem is shook.

Harry let go of the waist ribbon which he had been carelessly toying with, and clasped her graceful form to his breast while he imprinted kiss after kiss on her sweet lips. She blushed yet deeper, and faintly struggled to free her form from his passionate embrace, but it would have been plain to a less knowing man than Harry Whitmore, that her struggles were only dictated by an innate sense of propriety, not by her own natural inclinations.

But at last, even his ardor, as mere passion's ardor ever does, cooled off, and he used his lips once more for speaking.

"I now know that you *love* me, Isabella, and I am happy," said he—"happy to a certain degree, but I shall never be completely so until you are mine entirely, hand as well as heart!

She was about to speak, but he continued:

"I know not when this can be exactly, for we shall have one powerful opponent. My mother, upon whom I depend, is a very set woman, and she wishes me to marry a wealthy girl of her own choosing. She would disinherit me and cast me off for ever were I openly, and at once, to wed against her will."

"Why should she object to me. There is not one breath in all the world which can stain my character."

"I know that well, dear Isabella, but my mother is a very strange woman. It is to our interest, dear one, not to offend her."

"I do not wish to, Harry—no not to attain happiness for my-self. I am yours, at your own time !"

"Aye, and in my own way," said the heartless wretch, in a tone too low for her to hear, and then he added: "it will not be long, dear one. My sweet sister shall use her influence. Maria has heard of you so often through me, that she already knows and loves you. You must indeed see her, and to day."

"Whenever you like, Harry. I have now no will but yours."

"She comes into the traces right handsomely," muttered Har-ry again, and then while he imprinted another burning, passion-ful kiss on her pure lips, he said:

"I must leave you for a brief time, sweet one. I shall return within two or three hours, and then you shall visit my sister. If Charles comes home while I am out, tell him I will join him this evening as he desired; and by the way, Isabella, say nothing of our late conversation to him or to your mother. At a proper time I will break it to both of them !"

"It shall be as you wish," responded the young girl, but she wondered much why he should wish to keep this news from her only relatives. Her young heart was so full of joy that she wish-ed to pour out its over-running into the bosoms of those whom she loved. She yearned to tell her dear good mother that she *loved*, was *beloved*, and felt too happy for utterance. But for his sake, and regarding alone his wishes, she restrained herself.

Again he kissed her, and then arose and left her side.

He had not gone ten steps from the door, when he met his sha-dow, Gustave Livingston.

"I was just coming to find you Harry ; got some capital news for you !" cried the latter, as he met our arch villain.

"Well, Gus, out with it !"

"You remember the little mink that we tossed up for in front of Florence's, dont you ?"

"Yes, the sewing girl, you mean. I ought to remember her, when I got knocked down for her."

' I know where she is—where she lives !"

" Well, what of it ?"

" You seem rather cool about it—I suppose you wont even thank me for my information."

" I shall not—I've better game afoot than her !"

" Then you're willing to give her up to me?"

" Certainly. I don't want to see the dowdy thing again. If I hadn't been a little tipsey I should have never looked at her !"

" She's the prettiest girl I ever saw in Gotham !"

" What! prettier than my 'Bella ? It is impossible."

" It is true—but, speaking of her, how goes on the game ? Are you likely to win ?"

" Of course. Did you ever know me to lose in such a game. Did I ever lay my eyes on fruit which I failed to taste ?"

" Ah, Harry, you're a sad dog—a demnition sad dog ! Which way were you steering when I met you ?"

" Down to Greenwich street to see Maria. I've got to arrange matters for Isabella to meet my *sister ?*"

" *Your* sister ! Ha ! Ha ! a demed good joke ! Rich, exceedingly !"

" It will be if it is well carried through, but I must hurry along. I've no time to waste, for I've got to introduce Isabella, and then to return in time to meet Charley, and go with him to Carlton's They can skin him better there than at Pat's. Pat will be a gentleman in spite of his profession, and hasn't the heart to quite ruin a poor devil like Charley, but they'll do him up in the other place.'

" I shouldn't wonder if they did, for that genteel and polished scoundrel, Sam Selden, deals pretty often, and " Butcher Bill" is always on hand for a look-out and adviser."

" Well, meet me there at ten to-night, and we'll see what we can make. Carlton promises halves."

"I'll be there," replied Gus, and then the two separated ; one to prepare to ruin the pure and unsuspecting Isabella, the other, to persecute our poor Angelina. *Poor,* we said ; yes, that girl is poor in all things save virtue, patience and industry. We will soon pay her a visit, and in the meantime will take a cruise to Mr. Jack Circle's den, and see how the burglars are getting along.

CHAPTER II.

ONCE more in the upper back room of the crib, known in our first number as Jack Circle's, and located in Cherry street, near the Catherine Market.

Jack is there in all his glory, for he has a large party of his gang around him, who have come to report the labors of the past week, and to cut out new work for the next. Bill Hoppy, Bob Sutton, Black Bill and many others of our old friends are there. In the darkest corner, by the side of Harriet Circle, stands a young man dressed very neatly in black, whom the reader will recognise, because he is making love in most poetic language to the *lady*. It is none other than Frank Hennock. He was just in the middle of Romeo's garden address to Juliet, which he was slightly altering to suit Harriet's circumstances, when the meeting was called to order by Mr. Circle, who cried :

"Vel, my covies, ve might as vel perceed to business. Frank, my kiddy, vot 'ave you done in the vay of that 'ere lay I put you on."

"Not much as yet, Captain Jack!" replied the young hopeful. "I borrowed this five hundred from the old gentleman the other night at the Points," and the young villain handed over the pocket-book of Mr. Precise, from which he had taken the odd eleven dollars, to leave even hundreds.

Jack's eyes sparkled as he opened the dummy and looked at its contents. "Vy, my kiddy, you *is* one of the b'hoys, sure! You've paid your veek's hexpenses and summat more for yerself! 'Ows the old 'un's crib?"

"It would be very easily cracked—but I think we'd better hold on a while!"

"Vy, vots in the vay now?"

"Nothing in the way, only the prospect of a little heavier haul if we wait!"

"Jest 'ave the kindness to hexplain yerself, younker, 've doesn't deal in riddles."

" Why, my new master is expecting a fortune over from England very soon. He comes by his mother's side from the celebrated Hunt family, and the lawyers have hunted him up and only a little more proof is wanting to give him a whole million of bright dollars."

All the party now gathered up closer to Frank and listened with deep interest to his remarks.

"'Ow did you find out all o' this?" asked Jack.

"By the letters he receives and which I have to answer. Of course I know all his secrets, being his private secretary."

" Vel, my kiddy, ve'll see vots best. If there's a show for more than he's got now, ve'd better vait for it, for ve're a doin very vel 'on our other lays."

" Aye, and ve'll do better yet on a new von as I've clapped my peepers on !" cried Jack Shaw, giving a very knowing leer with his squint eye.

" Vot is it Jack?" asked old Circle—" You're allers on 'and, vith somethin' rich !"

" Vel if we gits into the crib that I was pattering about, we'll make one of *the* hauls, but it's a rather tight place—got alarm bells, big dog and all that !"

" If its got the swag in it, that's hall that ve asks !" said Bill Hoppy.

"Vel, it *has*, Bill, but 'ow about that ere gospel shop as you was agoin for to crack last week?" replied Shaw.

" All right as a trivet, my cove—took the pewter and old Jack smashed it for us."

" Yes," replied old Circle, " Ven ve counts up you'll see 'ow I've done it up. But 'ow about that 'ere Boston lay?"

Black Bill, to whom this question was propounded, replied:

" It vont do yet. I sent on to have the screws fitted, and somethin's leaked out, for they've put a glim inside and two he fellers and a dog. People is a gettin bright now a days; afore long a cracksman vont 'ave no more chance than a stump-tailed cow in fly time."

" That's a gospel fact," sighed Harriet, and she was about to say more when three double taps were heard at the door, signifying that some of the gang wished admittance.

"Let 'em in, 'Arriet, my gal!" said old Circle.

Harriet obeyed, and two persons entered. One was a tall, dark complexioned, shrewd looking fellow, in whose jet black eyes could be seen the fire of villainy and deep cunning. His arched eye-brows, aquiline nose, thin lips and curling black hair, all bespoke him a native of a foreign soil. In fact, he looked like a gipsey, or an Italian.

A woman was with him, and her features were so like his, that any one would know them to be brother and sister. She was younger and more delicate than he; rather pretty, and dressed very neatly and well. The man looked to be about thirty-five or forty years of age; he too was genteelly dressed.

As he entered he spoke, his accent also being evidence of his foreign derivation.

"All here, I see, Captain!" said he.

"Aye. 'Ow d'ye Genlis! 'ow's your sister! and 'ow goes on fortin telling?"

"Well," replied the man, "fools are more plenty here than in Europe, but they don't pay as well. I'm about to try a large game, however!"

"Vot's that? Pad your limber and let's ear vot it is!"

"Why I've got my eye on a child who shall make at least a hundred thousand dollars for us, in one way or another!"

"A kid? I don't understand you!"

"Well, I'll explain. I know a young married couple who are very rich. They have a child which they idolize. That child shall be stolen; by opportune hints, when they are driven to despair at its loss, they shall hear of Genlis the Gipsey fortune teller. They'll pay well to see their lost one, if it is only in my magic looking-glass. Then in one way or another, we'll skin them till they are worth a little less than nothing!"

"It 'll be a great lay, if the game 's fat," replied old Jack. "Is it a gold finch?"

"Fifty thousand, hard dust; more coming in every day and plenty of plate!" replied the Gipsey.

"Vere is it?" asked Jack Shaw, who had been listening to the words of Genlis.

"That's telling, my cove, I always keep dark when I don't want a pal, and my sister is all I need on this lay!" replied the Gipsey, casting a rather distrustful glance at the burglar.

"I honly axed caze I thought you'd spotted a crib that I 'ad my own peepers on up in the Third avenue," replied the thief, carelessly, but at the same time his keen eye was fixed upon the Gipsey's face, which for a moment wore an expression of surprise.

"Will you tell me the name of the family you mean?" asked Genlis.

"That 'ud be telling," replied the fellow, with a coarse laugh, at the idea of turning the tables on his non-communicative companion, and then he added : " I'd like to 'ave the dust that all that ere row of 'ouses would bring!"

"A row of houses! he certainly knows the place," said Genlis, in a low tone, then turning to Jack, he added—"If you've spotted the crib, Jack, I'll go you halves if I have my own way."

"D'ye think I'm sich a bloody noddy as all that 'ud come to?" replied the burglar. ".Why I've got two doors fitted now in the crib; it vould'nt take me a month o'Sundays to do the rest and go nobody halves."

"But I'll make more out of him than he's got in his safe, if it is Mr. Abingdon that you mean!"

"Vel, you 'ave hit it!" cried the burglar—"I thought ve vos on the same lay. Now ve can harrange the business!"

Leaving Jack Circle and his crowd for a little while, to fix and arrange their matters, we will take a glance at the characters who close the last chapter of the first number.

When Captain Tobin and his very select party reached Grand street, they passed up on its shady side until they reached Elizabeth street. Down this they turned a few steps and passed into a door which was kept by a Dutch porter who received one shilling from each, the usual admittance fee. As they entered, the sound of music greeted their ears, and to its time they could hear the sound of many a heavy foot upon the spring floor above. Ascending to the second story they entered an immense room, where at least twelve or fifteen hundred people were assembled.

Around the sides of this large room were rows of tables, at each of which were many sitters, who seemed to be very generally engaged in drinking and smoking.

A large brass band was manufacturing exceedingly loud music in a loft which overlooked the floor, and to this music at least one hundred and fifty couple were waltzing around the room, in a circle formed by a *core* of spectators who occupied the centre of the room. The company was mostly made up of Germans, especially the female portion of it. Many of these were servant girls; some were the wives and daughters of German mechanics and laborers; still others by their rouged cheeks and gaudy dresses told their miserable profession.

The room was very full, and when Captain Tobin looked in, he muttered to his companions:

"Zis is one ver grand push! If we shall neek ze right peoples, we shall make one ver gran speculatione!"

His keen eye caught sight of some young city bucks, who were mingling in with the check-aproned ladies, waltzing with some and drinking with others; and giving the wink to his party, he walked quietly forward to the place where the crowd stood thickest.

Preceded by the stutterer, who now pretended to be staggering drunk, a thing not at all unfashionable there, Captain Tobin passed on. Every now and then the stutterer would stagger up against some one, in a second he would feel the outer side of his pockets, and make a sign to his pal. At last he stumbled up against a very fat Dutchman, who was following the whirlpool of dancers with an admiring eye. A wink to Tobin, and then he managed to tread directly upon the fat gentleman's foot, which must have been gouty, for its owner bent forward and gave the stutterer a heavy push while he turned red with pain and cried:

"Got for tam! git off mine feet, you tam trunken hog!"

The stutterer's dignity was offended by this remark, and as he staggered back he planted his fist heavily between the offender's eyes, who reeled and fell back into the arms of Captain Tobin, who stood just behind him, ready to receive the victim.

"I'll l-learn you t-to insult a g-gent-gentleman!" cried the stutterer as he gave the blow.

When Tobin received the fat Dutchman in his arms, he bent over him with the greatest solicitude and cried:

"Mon Dieu, my ver dear sir, what shall zis mean? I nevare see such dam rascale, nevare! Are you ver much dam*age*, eh?"

"Got for tam! He preak mine feet first, den he preak mine head last!" muttered the Dutchman, as he regained his feet and looked around in vain for the stutterer.

"I am ver sorree for see such rascalitie biznasse!" said Captain Tobin sympathetically, "zat canaille villiane strike ver hard, eh?"

"Yaw—got for tam, yaw!" muttered the Dutchman, and then he added, "I musht rub mine head mit prandy!" and off he pushed his way toward the bar. Tobin stood still and watched him as he crossed the room, managing with great difficulty to steer clear of the dancers. Tobin saw him pass up to the bar, where he called upon one of the dozen pretty bar maids, who officiate, for some brandy.

The decanter was handed to him. He poured out a tumbler half full, then poured a very small quantity out in his hand which he applied to the spot where he received the blow. The rest he very speedily swallowed, thus proving himself an advocate for inward applications.

With a kind of malicious interest the French Captain had watched all of these movements, and he smiled as he saw the Dutchman put his hand down in his capacious trowsers pocket, to get the change necessary to pay for the liquor. As he did so, a look of surprise came over his full-moon face—then he felt in all his other pockets, each time a new change coming over his face. Tobin heard again the distant sound of his voice as he fiercely muttered—"Got for tam!" and then while the dexterous gnof patted his hand against his side pocket, he said:

"I sink I shall go and ask him that I shall lend him some monee for pay his liquor, eh? I sink I shall 'ave some gran sport wiz my speculatione!"

The Captain was about to go and rejoin the Dutchman, when

10

a low "hist" close by his ear made him turn around quickly, and he saw Big Lize and her pal close to him, the former leaning on the arm of a large, rather singularly dressed German, the pal in very close connection with the coat tail of the German, who was evidently making love to Lize! He was a tall, raw-boned large framed man, with about as much symmetry in form as there would be in a forked tree turned top downwards, and had a pair of pants which fitted his huge legs nearly as tight as the skin. He had a coat with very short tails and these seemed to have had a quarrel with each other—they were so far apart.

"What's the time, my lump o' honey?" asked Lize of her new found beau, at the same time glancing at a very pretty Geneva enammeled chain which he wore.

The German drew out a huge silver watch with which the delicate chain contrasted as would a ribbon with a log-chain, and gave her the hour. Her look of eagerness somewhat fell when she looked at his cheap coarse watch; but then the chain was worth having, and she had not yet ascertained whether he had money or not. To test this was her next step, and she proposed to her new cavalier to take her to the bar and treat her. To this he made no objections, and the whole party, including the French Captain, started toward the bar. Here, still stood our poor fat Dutchman quarrelling with one of the bar maids, she demanding the pay for the brandy, he swearing that his pocket had been picked, which she of course would not believe.

"What is ze mattere sare?" asked Captain Tobin with an air of kind solicitude, as he reached the side of the victim.

"Got for tam! Lose mine monee, prake mine head, stomp mine feet!"

"Lost your monee, eh? I shall lend you some sare? I ver sorree for you!" continued the captain.

The Dutchman looked at the speaker, then looked down in his hand wherein he held three or four dollars in change, and muttered, as he carefully picked out a sixpence from the rest and gave it to the bar maid,

"Tank you Mynheer! I gif it you 'gain!"

"Nevare mind, sare, nevare mind; will you not drink wiz me now?"

"Yaw! I pelieve I'll git trunk, I lose all my monee!"

"Ah, sare, I am ver sorree! How much 'ave you lose?"

"More as one huntred thalers, Got for tam!" muttered the fat Dutchman.

"Ah, zat is ver bad! ver much monee for zese bad times!" sighed the Captain, and then he renewed his invitation for the other to drink.

The German called for some schnaps, while the more refined Captain asked for claret. While they were drinking, a rich game was going on with the other German. Charley Cooper, who didn't seem to like his love making to Lize, appeared determined to have some fun, and while the German's back was turned toward a dark corner of the bar-room, he quietly and unobserved by any-body, took his keen nicking knife and severed both the coat tails of the German, leaving him only a round jacket, which was too short in the waist to improve his figure much. That he made a singular looking carricature of humanity now, the reader may well fancy.

The moment Charley succeeded in severing the nether extremities of the coat, he quietly slipped off with them concealed under his own large over-coat, into a still darker corner of the room, where, having rifled the pockets, he dropped them on the floor, and returned again to the scene of action.

Ere he could reach it, however, there was a terrible uproar in front of the bar. The tall German, after taking his schnaps, had wished to wipe the red moustache which hedged his upper lip, and had felt in vain for his pocket handkerchief, thereby discovering his loss. In a moment he was convulsed with rage, and his ridiculous appearance as he moved around, cursing in the choicest low Dutch, caused peals of laughter, from every one around him. He seized, first one and then the other, of those nearest to him, shouting,

"Gif me pack mine coat dails! gif me pack mine coat dails!" and was answered only by the shouts of laughter which came from every side. Every one thought it was a good joke, except the recipient thereof, who undoubtedly deemed himself a victim.

And he had more reason to think so, when in a few moments afterward a hand reached quickly in under his arm, from behind his back, and grasping his guard-chain tore it from his neck, breaking off the chain and dashing the watch to the floor. As he stooped to pick up the watch, some one from behind pushed him forward, and in a moment his huge foot was placed upon it, of course crushing it into atoms.

"Oh, Mein Got! Mein Got!" groaned the German, "mine coat is ruin, mine wash is proke, mine shain is rob; oh, Mein Got, Mein Got, de duyvel has come for me!"

The chain had been taken so suddenly and boldly that no one could imagine who had taken it, and now the row began to increase every moment. Every one was afraid of his next neighbor, and many a hand was seen clasping firmly the pockets of its owner.

Finding every one on their guard and the place getting rather warm, Captain Julian Tobin gave the signal to his party to retire, but they had been gone a considerable time before anything like order was restored, and it is probable that the sufferers are yet mourning their losses; especially he whose *tale* had been made so brief by the relentless knuck.

CHAPTER III.

The widowed mother of Angelina, our poor sewing girl, sat alone in her cellar. A cheerful fire was burning before her; there was food upon the barrel-table, by which she had been at work. The night was just setting in, but the bright fire-light precluded the necessity of a candle, especially as the old lady was not sewing.

She had a glad expression on her worn and wasted countenance; it seemed to be as much a stranger there too, as a tear would be upon a stern warrior's cheek. She was soliloquizing, and as she spoke, she shook silver in her hand, as a kind of accompaniment to her words.

"God is good!" she said. "It is strange why this good young man should take so much interest in me, who are so poor, who beforetime have been neglected by all. He gave me five dollars in bright silver, and sent me food and fuel, and says I shall no longer live in a cellar. How good and noble he is. Angelina will be so happy when she comes—for now the poor girl can rest."

At this moment, she of whom the mother spoke, entered. Her little hood and shawl were both spotted over with the snow which was falling outside, and the long curls of her hair were filled with the large flakes. She staggered as she entered, and tottered over to the bed whereon she half reclined, and murmured:

" Give me some water, dear mother—I am very weary, and my head aches with a deep and throbbing pain, which dims my eyesight. My cheeks burn, feel how hot they are, and yet it is cold in the air." The poor girl closed her eyes, and sunk back still more.

The mother hastily took up a bottle which stood by the food, and pouring out some of its contents into a broken tea-cup, hurried to her daughter's side, raised her head, and after removing her hood, held the cup to her lips.

"Drink my poor child, drink ; it will do you good !" said she, tenderly.

The young girl opened her lips, but as she took one swallow of the draught, she raised her head and looking her mother in the face with a wondering eye, said

"That is not water, mother !"

"No, my child, it is wine. Drink it, it will make you strong; I drank some before you come, and feel *so* smart now !"

"Wine, mother? I have heard that rich people drank wine—how did you get any ?"

"A good young man came here just after you went down to the store with the finished work, and he seemed to feel so much for us. He brought me some food and wood, and gave me five dollars in money !"

"What for, mother? Did he want work?"

"No, child, no. He was rich, and he had a gentle heart. He saw our poverty, and you see how kind he has been.

The girl looked at the food, the cheerful fire, and then her large blue eyes filled with tears.

"For your sake, I am very glad mother !" she murmured.

"For my sake, child? Why not for your own, too?'

"Because I shall not stay long, mother, to see it. I have had a fever for more than a week, and it is killing me.'"

"Oh, no, dear, dear child !" cried the mother—"it is not, cannot be so. Here take some of this wine, you will soon feel better !"

"I'd rather have water, mother—the wine burns my lips, and they are too hot now !"

"You shall have it, poor dear. Yes, your cheeks are hot and red too as roses !"

The good mother hurried to the broken pitcher which stood beside the work table, and brought it to her daughter. The girl took a long draught from the pitcher and then murmured :

"Pour out a little in your hand, mother, and put it upon my forehead, for my head aches dreadfully !"

The parent did as she was desired. With her thin hands she laved the pale brow of her sick child, and pushed back the golden tresses for fear of wetting and dimming their glossiness, for indeed they were beautiful.

As the poor girl revived more, she reached out her hand, which she had kept close clenched until now, and said:

"There is the dollar for our last three days work, mother. I'm glad you have more—but this we *earned*."

There was a faint tone of pride in her voice as she spoke. That tone seemed almost like a rebuke to her mother for having accepted charity, but the latter heeded it not, for she said:

"That dollar will buy you a pair of shoes, dear, the ones you have on are entirely worn out, and we have money enough to rest now for a whole week at least !"

"I'd rather do something else with the dollar, mother, if you'll give it to me !"

"What, my child ? Surely you need shoes more than anything else."

"I can do without them, mother, but the ring that my poor father gave to me when he was dying, we pawned it, you know, for a dollar, and I have never been happy since. It had his coat of arms on it, and he told me never to lose it, for by it we might find our uncle out if ever he came back from England."

"True, child, but we've been so poor I had forgotten that."

"I never have, mother. I'd like to see my uncle before I die."

"Oh don't talk of dying, child, my heart is half broken now; don't speak of dying !" and the mother burst into a flood of tears.

The angel daughter drew her mother's head down upon her bosom and kissed her eyes, while she said soothingly:

"Don't cry, dear mother, I'll not speak of death again—I'll try not to think of it !"

Then as the mother became once more calm, she added:

"Uncle had a daughter—my cousin, hadn't he ?"

"Yes, child, but she was very bad and almost broke his heart. He killed her seducer and fled to England. I have never heard of him since !"

"Where is *she*—his daughter ?"

"I don't know, dear. I once heard that she was living a terrible life, but I wouldn't believe it. I should rather have hoped that she was dead."

"*Dead*, mother?"

"Yes, child; rather than see *you*, where I last heard she was, I would pray God to let you die. I would rather close your eyes for the last time, than open mine to see your infamy."

"Don't talk so, mother. You need never fear for your child. She can die, but she will never do wrong."

"I know it, dear one—but won't you try and eat some? I have waited all this time for you to come home to eat with me."

"I cannot eat, mother; I am not hungry now. Oh, I would like to sleep, for my head aches *so* hard!"

"You shall, child, you shall, but not quite yet, for that good young gentleman is coming back again to see us to-night, to tell me where he will find us a better room than this!"

"What makes him so kind, mother?"

"His good heart, I suppose, child; what foolish questions you do ask?"

Not so foolish as the mother thought was that young girl's question. She had lived long enough in this all-selfish world of ours to know that few good acts are performed without some self-interested cause; though we will do the *few* justice who act without selfishness. They are as angel visitants, upon the earth, "few and far between."

Immediately after the mother had responded to Angelina's question, a tap was heard at the door, and while the daughter arose from the bed and took off her shawl, the mother hastened to open the door.

When she did so, a person who stood outside, close muffled in a cloak, entered. As he did so, and opened his cloak, the old lady exclaimed:

"I thought it was he. This, Angelina, dear, is our benefactor!"

Angelina had started to her feet, and when she did, her fever-hued cheeks and excited eyes gave her an almost supernatural beauty, but when she glanced at him who entered, her color faded, she bent down her head and hid her face.

"What is the matter, child? Why do you not look up and speak?" asked the mother. "This is the gentleman, dear, who has been so kind to us?"

"Oh, mother, I have seen him before. He was one of those who insulted me on that dreadful night, when I ran all the way home!"

The mother had no time to speak, for *Gus. Livingston* stepped forward and said:

"It is true, madam, that I met your beautiful daughter when I was rather the worse for liquor. But I did not know how good and pure she was, or I would rather have died than injured her."

He said this in a tone so kind and earnest, that the mother was completely won over to his side.

"I am sure you would'nt, sir," said she, "I know that you are too good-hearted to do her harm, who never has harmed you."

"Indeed, I hope I am, madam. That I once had a share in frightening her, is true, but I offer an humble apology; and to prove that I am your friend and her's rather than an enemy, I have come to say that you will find a large furnished room engaged in a house, No. — Leight street, to which you can move in the morning. The room is paid for a month in advance, and here is ten dollars more to settle up with here, and to move you."

"God bless you for your kindness, sir," said the old lady, "you are too generous. I do not need half so much. I owe nothing here except this week's rent, one dollar!" and the old lady tried to hand him back the golden eagle which he had placed in her hand.

"No, no, my good madam, no, keep it!" said he, "you are clothed but too scantily for the season, keep it for your necessities. You are poor, I am rich, compared with you, keep it for my sake!"

The widow wept, while she consigned it to woman's usual pocket—that formed by the portion of her dress which covers her heart, we mean—and then she remembered that she had not asked the gentleman to sit down. She hurriedly wiped the seat of one of the low stools with the skirt of her dress, and placing it before the fire, asked him to occupy it.

"No, no, my kind madam," said Gus, with a patronizing air,

"I only called to let you know where I had secured a better lodging for you; but I am sorry that your sweet daughter seems so unforgiving."

"Oh, she is not so, sir. The poor girl is sick and fretful. You will find her grateful, sir, indeed you will, when you meet us again."

"I hope that she will be less sad and more forgiving than now, at least!" replied Livingston, while he fixed his burning glance upon her as she sat, still pale and trembling, upon the bedside.

"Oh, she will be, indeed, sir, forgive her to-night. The poor girl is feverish. She has worked so hard all this fall and winter!"

"Poor creature, I pity her, indeed I do. She shall not again suffer so much!" said Gus, and both his look and tones were full of sympathy.

Angelina still sat with her head bent down, and her cheeks were yet pale. Livingston evidently saw that he could make no headway on that evening, and after giving the widow the number of the room which he had engaged for her, and the receipt for its rent, he took his leave, promising to visit her in her new quarters on the next evening.

"Why did you act so coldly, Angelina, to the gentleman? I've a great mind to be angry—to be very angry with you, child!" said the widow, when herself and daughter were left alone. Her tone was stern, far more so than usual.

Angelina burst into tears.

"Oh, mother, it is hard to hear you speak so harshly. That man means no good by all this kindness. I see it all now, you will but too soon!"

"Oh, tush, child! You are too suspicious. What could induce him to act selfishly?"

"Too much, mother. I am young, and to my misfortune, they think me beautiful!"

"They're right, child! You are pretty, though you are my daughter, and I say it. You are very handsome. Who knows but what this noble young gentleman will fall in love with you and marry you?"

"*Marry* me, mother? *He* marry me! Oh little do you know of him or his class, if you think he would marry me.

The snake charms the bird to destroy the fledgeling in its nest. He is the snake, you are the bird, I am the fledgeling."

"Oh, tush, child! You speak in riddles. But your cheeks are flushing up with the fever again; you had better go to bed!"

"I will, mother, after I have prayed God to care for us in this new danger!"

"Well, child. We will sleep early to-night, that we may rise soon in the morning and go to a better room. But I *must* eat, I'm very hungry."

"Do not wait for me, mother, I am hungry no more!" and the daughter with this sank to her knees by the side of the little cot, while the mother seated herself to her cold supper.

CHAPTER IV.

THE reader remembers that hell which we described as being appropriately situated, in that it overlooked a grave-yard. We will give him now a scene within that place, and show him some of the demons who there do congregate.

We will pass by the supper table; we will not even glance at the rich paintings and costly furniture, but will at once take a place before the gambler's altar—the *faro* table.

Look at the two most important personages behind it; the banker and the dealer. The first, is a man of middle size, slender, well formed, and very genteelly apparelled. He has a blue eye, regular features, light brown hair, and a still lighter beard and moustache. His face is very pale, and there is an expression of care and anxiety upon it, which speaks of some hidden sadness. He sits upon the right hand of the dealer, and attends to the cashing of checks, and the checking of cash.

He is none other than the husband of the lady whom we have described as dwelling in the suite of rooms above—Mr. Henry Carlton.

Now, for one glance at the dealer. You have seen Mr. Sam Selden before, and in the very chapter which described this place. He is now in his glory, for the faro box is in his hands, and verdant victims are before him—but his look is cold and careless, for they are but a picayune set, who are playing; young clerks, and boys who are only losing their pocket money. To win this, is only to keep up the game, till something better turns up.

But see! the cold look of Mr. Selden melts into a sweet and fascinating smile; his dark eyes flash with pleasure, and in a low whisper, he tells Carlton that " the pigeon is coming."

A party of three advance from the other room, and as they

come in, Carlton arises, and stretching out his hand to Harry Whitmore, says :

"How are you this evening, my dear sir? I'm exceedingly pleased to see you and your friends here. Mr. Meadows how do you do? Walk into the other room a few moments, and take some supper and a glass of wine; in the mean time, we'll manage to make our table a little more exclusive."

The young men did as they were desired; and soon the report of a champagne cork announced that they had obeyed directions. An half hour later, and the young men arose from table, much higher spirited than when they sat down, and re-entered the faro room.

It was now only occupied by about a dozen persons, and all these were of that class called sporting *gentlemen*. The other customers, whose games were too light for profit, had been reminded that it was one o'clock, and time to close, they had therefore absented themselves.

"We can have a cosy, genteel game, now, Charley!" said Harry Whitmore, as he seated himself with his two companions, directly before the dealer. The other replied:

"I hope it will be a more winning one than the last I played."

His look and tone were both a little gloomy as he spoke; but as others seemed to notice this, he assumed a gayer tone, and addressing himself to Carlton, cried:

"We intend to run you hard to night, sir. We've brought a *pile* amongst us, on purpose to break the bank."

There was a singular smile on the banker's face, when he replied:

"We'll have to stand our luck, what ever it is. Fortune is more fickle than woman!"

Meadows was about to reply, but Selden, who had been "fixing" the cards, now cried:

"Make your bets, gentlemen! deal's ready!"

The countenance of Meadows became a shade paler as he drew out a large roll of bank notes from his pocket-book, and laid them down by his right hand. The eyes of the gamblers sparkled all the brighter, when they noted the *hundred* marks upon the bills and saw that he intended to " play large." They too, to keep up appearances, began to have their fives and tens changed into checks, and placed their bets also on the table.

"Shall I give you some checks?" asked Carlton of Meadows.

"No, sir! I will play a larger game than that!" and as he spoke he placed three one hundred dollar bills on a single card.

Harry Whitmore bet a twenty dollar bill on the same card, and Gus. Livingston followed suit with a five.

"All down?" asked Mr. Sam Selden, with a quiet glance at each face around the table.

No answer being given, the affirmative was assumed, and the deal commenced.

Charles Meadows tried to appear calm, but the color began to heighten in his face, his lips began to quiver and his hand to tremble.

The deal went on. The ace, whereon Charles had laid his money, won and his bet was doubled. Of course Gus. and Harry also won, and the two latter at once took up their bets and winnings. Not so with their reckless friend. His game was evidently desperate and he let his six hundred remain upon the card.

The deal again went on, and again that ace won, leaving twelve hundred dollars on the card. The excitement of Meadows now became intense. The pupils of his eyes dilated—the color came and went in his face as the flushes of the Aurora Borealis flit across a northern sky. Thrice he moved his hand to take up the money—but he withdrew it again, and in a stern tone cried:

"Go on with your deal! it shall be all or nothing!"

The others all stopped to see his play and the deal went on. Again, for the fourth time, that card won.

Twenty-four hundred dollars were now his own, and it seemed as if he should have been satisfied, but he was not, for in a tone of triumph, he cried:

"I told you I'd run you hard, Carlton!"

"Yes," replied the latter, with a dissembled appearance of chagrin, "you do seem to be in luck to-night!"

"I am, and it is high time that I was. I've lost enough within the last two weeks to drive a man mad! Shuffle for a fresh deal, while I take a glass of that old brandy to steady my nerves. I'll show you how to bet now, fellows!"

The moment that Charles turned his back to go to the side-board, Carlton bent his head over to Harry, and in a whisper asked:

" How large is his pile, to-night?"

" Five thousand, he told me, just before he came in!"

A smile was exchanged between the two, and the next moment Charles returned, having swallowed a bumper of brandy.

"All ready, again!" cried the polished Selden. "Make your bets, gentlemen; make your bets!"

All declined; saying, that it was now a battle between Meadows and the bank, and they preferred looking on to engaging in the game.

The dealer still remained calm and composed, and fingered the cards as cooly as if thousands were not depending upon their turn. The deal commenced afresh, Charley again betting upon the ace.

The cards were turned up—he lost, at one sweep, all of his winnings. He took from the roll of bills in his pocket-book exactly the same amount—laid it again upon the ace. A second time it lost. He had now but twenty-three hundred dollars left. With that recklessness which blind despair only can give, he laid down two thousand dollars upon that fatal ace. Mr. Sam Selden smiled as he saw this; one quick moment of the villain's dexterous fingers and again the ace was turned upon his own side.

"Your luck has turned!" remarked Carlton in a low tone, "you had better wait for another chance!"

" I think I will; yes, sir, I think I *will!*" responded the young man in a hollow voice, with a calmness which was supernaturally strange, because it was forced.

Then he turned to his companions:

" Let us go on a spree? Let's have a regular bender—I've three hundred left, and it'll just put us through fair!"

" Where shall we go?" asked Harry.

" To Jule's, or to hell! I don't care where, so there's plenty of liquor to be had! Harry Whitmore, if you knew what I know to-night, you'd —— no I won't say it!"

"Won't say what, Charles, my dear fellow?" replied Harry, "what is the matter? You look wild! Are you ill?"

"No—no! I was only thinking. It's nothing now—but I had a strange fancy. Did you ever see a man shot?"

"Shot?"

"Yes, in this way, just so!" cried the young man, and quick as thought he drew a pistol from his pocket, cocked it, placed it against his temple, and pulled the trigger.

Harry and Livingston sprang instantly to his side, but had the weapon exploded, their movement would have been too late. As it was the cap merely burst, but the unfortunate young man gasped, murmured:

"Eternal disgrace! my poor sister and mother!" then fell back senseless on the floor. The excitement had been too much for him—the wretched youth had fainted.

"We must not carry him home in this state? where can we put him till he recovers?" said Harry, as he helped to raise the young man from the carpet, and took the pistol which Charles still held with a convulsive clutch.

"I have a room up stairs," replied Carlton, "where he can be taken care of for the present, and I will send for my own doctor. He is used to such cases, and knows how to treat them.

The party now broke up. Harry Whitmore assisting to carry Charles up to the bed-room which Mr. Carlton offered for the use of his victim.

Whitmore sent Livingston away, but remained himself, saying that he would watch over his friend till daylight. After the doctor came, Selden, Carlton and Harry left the room for a few moments, and returned to the bank to divide the *plunder*.

"How much has he got out of his old man, now ;—old S——, I mean?" asked Carlton, alluding to Charles.

"About fourteen or sixteen thousand, I think! It is hard to find out, for he does not know that I am aware of his defalcations."

"Well, there is plenty more to be had, if he only plays his game right—I think I shall have to advise him, somewhat!"

"Well, do anything that don't commit me. I've a game to

play with his sister, which must not be blocked, till it is through !"

"Ah, you're a sad dog among the women !" said Selden, with an approving smile—"I'm lucky myself, but you run me out of sight, in that line."

"Never mind the women—they're a curse to a man at the best !" cried Carlton, "let us talk of this business. After we get all we can out of old S——, through this pigeon, I want to use him in another way. I'll set Jack Circle and his gang to work, and with this fellow's knowledge, we can make a clean sweep of the whole establishment."

"What !—are you connected with him ? I never dreamed that you were quite so extensive in your villainy !" cried Whitmore. in a tone of surprise.

Carlton frowned, but simply replied :

"You've a great deal to learn yet, sir ! but we'll put off this matter till to-morrow, and then have a regular understanding in the case."

Harry now returned to his friend's side, and the others retired to their rooms.

11

CHAPTER V.

On a bed in his neat, second-story back chamber, lay Mr. Precise. He had been very sick, with an inflamatory rheumatism, caught with a severe cold, at the time when he returned to his house, on foot, from the Five Points, without his over-coat, which the reader will remember he took off to cover the sick woman in the Brewery.

A large writing table was drawn close up to his bed-side, and before this sat Frank Hennock, pen in hand, busily writing. Numerous letters lay before him, and as from time to time he referred to these, it was presumptive that he was responding to them.

It was near night, so near that Mr. Precise said :

"You had best light a candle, Francis. It will hurt your eye-sight to write in the twilight. Thank God, candles are plenty, and it is better to consume them than the sight."

Frank answered only by arising and obeying the wish.

Again seating himself, he was about to resume his work, when Mr. Precise interrupted him by asking :

"Who was that gentleman that you named to me to-day, Francis, as a good lawyer ; one who could be entrusted with the legal matters regarding the inheritances of the Hunt family ?"

"Mr. Tarhound, sir. He is a very smart man—(in his own opinion.") The last four words were uttered *sotto voce*.

"I think I'd like to see him Francis. My head is completely turned topsy turvy with this business. I sometimes wish that I hadn't a drop of the Hunt blood in my veins, or that the family had never left any property !"

The old gentleman was unusually petulant as he said this, for his body was racked with pain. A twinge came over him as he made the last expression, and while it made him writhe under its torture, his red face turned to even a darker purple. But it passed away, and he became more calm.

"I was wrong to make that last wish !" said he, " very wrong, for I want this money. Yes, I *need* it very much !"

"You in *need*, sir ?" exclaimed Frank.

" Yes, my good boy ; not for myself, but for others. Have you forgotten the misery we saw but a few nights since !"

" Oh, no, sir, nor can I ever forget it."

"' I don't think you can, my boy—indeed I don't. I wish now to be rich, Francis, to be very rich, so that I can help these poor wretches. I've a plan in my head, which I've been thinking of all the day long, to save and benefit them."

" What is it, sir, if you please ?"

"It is this, Francis. When my share of the Hunt estate comes to me, if it is two or three hundred thousand dollars, as they say it may be, I will buy a large farm, eight or ten miles from the city, and put up plenty of houses and work-shops. I will call it the "HOME OF THE POOR." You shall help me to manage its affairs, for I will be at its head, and we will go and pick up all these poor people and take them there. I will be very particular, Francis, in the government. There shall be no drinking, no dissolute conduct. The women shall have a separate department, except those who are married, and they shall be taught to sew, and do other work. The men shall work the farm, raise their own food ; or such as are mechanics, shall have tools and employment. All of the money arising from their labor above their simple expenses, shall belong to those who earn it, and for them I will keep a kind of savings bank. I will have a school for the children, and they shall be brought up and educated under my own inspection. Those who have been wicked, shall never hear the past alluded to. Their crimes shall be forgotten, and all encouragement shall be given to them to live in the right way. I will have prizes for those who behave well—I will kindly reason with those who do not."

" It would be a great blessing, sir," said Frank, who had been gravely listening to the good old man's plan, " especially if that principle of not keeping up the memory of the past to the wretched, should be carried out. There are good asylums for the wretched in this city, but they seldom reform any one, because, either by direct words, careless hints, or thoughtless airs of superiority, they crush the spirit back into the very mire it is struggling to arise from."

"It is true. How well you reason, my good boy. You are the very one I need, Francis, in this great work. I wish to accomplish it : to see it succeed, and to know that I have saved some miserable creatures, from despair and crime; to see them happy, industrious and prosperous around me, and then I will be willing to die. Yes, to calmly go up to that God who will reward those who do their *duty* here below.

"You can go on with your letters, Francis. I'll think this matter over, while you are writing."

"If you please, sir, I should like to go and see my mother ! She was not very well last evening, when I was there !" replied the young man.

"Well, well, you may go, but be back early. You're a good boy—you love your mother. I like you for it, Francis, I do, indeed !"

Frank carefully filed his letters again, wiped his pen, and placed it across the top of his inkstand, and laid everything in its place upon the table, before he arose. Mr. Precise watched every motion, and a quiet smile lighted up his face as he saw how well the youth followed the lessons he had taught him.

"Go to the safe, Francis—here, take the key from under my pillow," said the old gentleman, "and take an eagle from a little tin box which contains just a hundred of them, and give it to your mother from me, to buy her warm clothes with. It is a very cold winter."

"Oh, you are too good, sir; too good !" said Francis, in a tone of grateful feeling, but he took the key and went for the money.

While this good old man was laying there, even amid his own sufferings and pains, planning ways of benefiting those who are ever to be found in this city, there were misers counting their gold, and clinging to it as fondly as ever a husband did to his long-loved, tried and cherished bride.

Yes, there were old men, who though on the very point of leaving this world on a voyage where they can carry no cargo, not even their shrivelled carcasses, counted and gloated over their gold, as if it could save their souls from perdition, their bodies from the worm. And were a naked, sick and life-weary beggar to ask these men for alms, their answer would be colder far than the wintry blast. Look at one of them.

This is a picture of what *is !* Look at it, ye close-fisted, griping, money-loving *wretches;* I can call ye nothing else, while I see daily and nightly the miseries which you have the *means* to relieve, and yet will not.

If you feel any wish to enter Heaven, just pave your way there by charity. It is the best road that I can point out to you, and has bridges in it, that will carry you over a multitude of sins.

CHAPTER VI.

ONE week can make a strange change in a beautiful being. It can fade the rose-hued cheek; it can dim the lustrous eye; it can shadow the lily brow; and oh, what may it not do with the heart, for from that comes all these changes.

In the very room where we last saw her, in that singular house, with the back-alley entrance, stood Mary Sheffield. Her cheek was pale, her eyes were sunken, her lips blue and quivering with excitement. The hand in which she held a crushed letter was trembling like the wing of a dying dove; her whole frame seemed quaking with excitement.

With her left hand pressed to her brow as if to still some throbbing pain, she paced to and fro across the room; her right hand clenched the letter.

"Oh God! has it come to this!" she moaned in a low tone of agony. "Deceived—betrayed—ruined! He writes that he is married—*writes*, to break the shock of our meeting. Oh, Heaven! —shall I not *curse* him? No; let Heaven avenge me. He will be here soon and will he dare to look upon her whose doom he has sealed; whose life he has blasted?"

A light tap at the door. Mary turned towards it, and stood pale, still as a marble statue. She spoke not; but with a powerful effort, seemed to still down the tempest in her heart.

The door was opened, and he whom we last saw with her, Albert Shirley, entered. Hastily he crossed the room, and with open arms advanced to embrace the lady.

Then for the first time she moved and spoke.

"Back, sir, keep back! Lay not your hand upon my form, lest it freeze!" and with an air of queenly dignity, she motioned him off with the same hand which held his letter.

"What does this mean, dear Mary?" asked the gentleman in

a tone of surprise—"I expected tears and reproaches from you --but not this icy coldness !"

"Tears, sir ! Can you, like Moses, draw water from a rock? Can sap come from a blasted tree? Oh, God! Albert Shirley, how can you, how dare you look upon her whom you have *ruined !*"

"Ruined, Mary! oh, speak not so! I will not desert you—I will save you !"

"Save me? From what? The poor-house, or the common brothel? Will you condescend to make me that which I *am* and yet dare not name, and make me an abettor in your adultery? Albert Shirley, I can die, but we must part—for ever ! Go to her whom you have injured—your *wife ;* but when you press her to your breast, remember how you have wronged me. Albert, you will have my blood to answer for before the bar of God—for my hours are told !"

"No--no, *dear* Mary. Do not speak so. I will do all that I can for you. Your beauty led me to this—I will do all that I can to repair it."

"You know my situation?" As the young girl asked this, her cheeks burned with a momentary blush, but it passed away in a moment, and left her even paler than before.

"Yes," he replied, "I do, and already have I made arrangements which will save you the shame of an exposure, and preserve your reputation."

"What are they ?"

"Whenever you call with this card, upon Madame Sitstill, whose number is also on it, she will do all for you that is necessary. She will be kind to you as a mother, and I have given orders for every comfort that money can command."

The girl stood and looked at him while he thus spoke, with an expression of such utter despair and misery, that if he had been possessed of a heart of stone, he would have felt it.

He did, and in a kind, imploring tone, he said :

"Dear Mary—do listen to and believe me. Come, sit down by me—let me hold your poor head on my breast, and once more kiss your brow."

Listlessly, even as if she had been an automaton, she suffered herself to be led to the sofa, when he seated himself by her side. She shrunk from him, when he put his arm around her waist, and after he had kissed her upon the forehead, she turned away her head with an involuntary shudder.

"Let us talk calmly, dear Mary," said he—"what *is*, cannot be helped. Shelley says, 'what 'twas weak to do, 'tis weaker to regret, once being done.' Cheer up; tell me of what you are thinking."

"*Only* of *murder*, sir!" responded the pale girl, still keeping her face turned from him.

"Murder, Mary! What do you mean?"

"Have not you asked me to commit a murder?"

"No—no, child. Call not the necessary act of which we have spoken, a murder. If that was a murder, hundreds of such crimes are committed every month in this city."

"It *is* a murder—it may prove a double murder, for I cannot endure much now!"

"Do not fear, dear Mary. There is no danger under such experienced hands as Mrs. S. Do you consent to go to her?"

"Oh, God! what can I do? I *must*, for if it is hard to bear alone the knowledge of my own shame, how could I endure the finger of scorn from others."

"It is true, Mary. For your own sake—for mine, do as I desire. When shall I have a room engaged for you?"

"Oh, not now. I cannot yet leave my place. I am pledged to give one month's notice before I leave my situation. Give me time to become prepared for the horrible suffering which I know I must endure."

"You shall have it, Mary. It will be time enough this three months yet."

"Then, in the mean-time, promise never to see me again!"

"Never to see you, Mary! Oh, cruel, cruel girl! You know not how I love you, or you would not act so!"

"*Cruel!* Albert Shirley you are the last being on earth to talk to me of *cruelty*. Have I not perilled and lost all that is precious to a woman, for your sake? Cruel! let the tiger which tears the poor gazelle, talk to it of cruelty, or the hawk which rends the bosom of the dove. MAN, no longer, my love—FARE WELL !"

Before the astonished Shirley could rise to his feet, she had snatched her bonnet, veil and shawl from the arm of the sofa, and darted from the room.

He knew that it was useless to follow her—and after going as far as the door, returned to the sofa. He sighed heavily as he re-seated himself.

"She is a strange creature !" he muttered in soliloquy. "If I could have made her my wife, she would have been the most true and devoted one that ever blessed a husband. But that was impossible. I do not wish to lose her, either. She is a magnificent girl. I hope she will be prudent—and perhaps after this first burst of passion is over, she will come back to quiet reason, and be as I wish her."

Oh, little did that man know of Mary Sheffield's heart, when he thought that her feelings, because quickly aroused, must be fleeting and changeable. There is a mine in a western mountain, a mine of coal, which fifty years ago was set on fire, by a light accidentally coming in contact with a current of gas. That mine caught in an instant—yet it has burned ever since. Where there is fuel in the heart, the flame of feeling may be lighted in an instant, and still it can burn *for ever*.

After his few words of soliloquy, Shirley arose and rang a little silver bell which was on the centre table.

The same lady of whom he made inquiries, as described in the eleventh chapter of our first part, answered the bell by her own appearance.

Shirley handed her a ten dollar bill, and bade her good day: then departed.

"Pretty good room-rent, for a half hour !" said the woman, with a smile, as she glanced at the bill. "Mary must have been very kind, to make him so generous."

Little did that woman dream of the scene which had just occurred in that room.

CHAPTER VII.

In the front parlor of the "355" house alluded to, by Harry Whitmore and Maria Deloraine in the thirteenth chapter of our first part, sat the female who we have last named.

From time to time, she glanced at the gold watch which she carried, and each moment her manner betrayed her impatience. She was seated by the centre-table, which was covered with periodicals and annuals. She had already glanced at the titles of every one of these, and looked at some of the engravings in them, but she seemed too nervous to appreciate or care for them.

She was there, waiting the arrival of Harry Whitmore, and Isabella Meadows, prepared to assume the character of Harry's sister. Her nervousness was very natural. Why should not a woman be excited who was taking her first step as an accomplice in the intended ruin of a pure and helpless girl.

She arose, went to the window, and slightly pushed aside the heavy crimson curtains, that she might look out into the street. As she did this, the door bell rang, and an expression of satisfaction passed over her face.

"They have come," she said, and then she hurried to her seat, and took up a book, which she opened in the middle, so as to appear deeply engaged.

The next moment the door opened, and Harry entered. Isabella was leaning on his arm. As Maria arose, Whitmore advanced, and introduced the two.

"Maria, this is Miss Meadows, of whom I have often spoken to you;—Isabella, know my sister!"

Maria at once sprang forward with an appearance of glad surprise, and kissing Isabella warmly, said:

"I have heard Harry speak of you so often that I know you

already. You've been bewitching him, I fear. He is ever talking of you."

The young girl blushed, and as she returned the kisses of Maria, with interest for the same, replied:

"I am glad to know that he remembers me when absent from my side."

"That is the time, dearest," said Harry, "when one who loves, thinks most of her to whom he is devoted, because then he most misses her. You know the old song—''tis said that absence conquers love,' &c., yet it is not so. But, Isabella, you must excuse me. I've some business in Wall street to attend to. I'll leave you with Maria, and return in an hour, or less."

When the two females were alone, the thread of their conversation was again renewed.

"My brother loves you, very much, Isabella."

"And I love him, too, very much!" replied the artless girl, coloring, however, as she spoke.

"So he has told me. He wishes to marry you immediately, but we are so situated with mother, that I fear he would be imprudent in doing so. He has told you all, I suppose?"

"He has only told me that she was a stern woman of strong prejudices!"

"Has he not told you that I do not live with her?"

"No, indeed, he has not!" replied Isabella, in a tone of surprise.

"It is true. This is the house of a friend, where I am boarding for the time. My mother quarrelled with me, and I determined to accept the offer of a kind friend, and to come here, and live with her until my mother became more reasonable."

"I am so sorry to hear of trouble existing between a parent and her children. I have the dearest, best mother in all the world. You must come and see her. I know you'll love her."

"I will, if she is like her daughter."

"Oh, she is far, far better!" replied the simple, pure-hearted creature, "and I know she will like you, even as I do!" and Isadella drew her chair close up to Maria, and clasping her arms around her neck, kissed her tenderly.

The cheek of the latter was for the first time, for many a day covered with blushes. Did not the fire of shame fill her heart, and cause them? Shame, that she should be an accomplice in the intended ruin of that pure and spotless creature. She could not even return the kisses which she received; her whole frame quivered as with the tremors of a troubled spirit, beginning to be irresolute in its very guilt.

"It cannot be—it must not!" she murmured, in a tone not intended for Isabella's ear. But they were heard by the latter, for she said:

"What do you allude to? Have you any trouble, dear sister? Forgive me; but I must call you *sister!*"

"Oh, Isabella, do not call me *sister!* Do not, for the sake of the heaven which made you pure, and me—— !"

What Maria Deloraine would have said, we know not. At that instant, the door opened, and Harry Whitmore re-entered the room. He saw the flushed countenance, and agitated manner of Maria, and in a moment divined that something was wrong. There was a momentary flash of suspicion in his heart, and anger in his eye, but he controlled it, and said in a gay tone:

"You've got the blues again, sister? You musn't mind these fits of sadness, Isabella. Sis will have them at times; but she is generally happy."

"Oh, yes, *very* happy! Happy as the death doomed prisoner. Happy as a dying infidel, who feels there is a God, but not for him!" replied Maria, bitterly.

"Oh, do not talk so, my dear sister! You shall be happy—Henry and me will make you so!" cried Isabella, trying to sooth the agitation of the other with caresses.

"Henry—I—yes, *we* are trying to make *you* happy! Are we not Henry? Shall I not tell her how much we intend to do for her?"

"Hush! as you value your life, hush!" whispered Harry, as he bent down and pretended to kiss her, and then as he saw she was about to speak, again he added, "if you speak, she shall never leave this house. You *know* me!"

The face of the girl turned pale—but it was with pain, for all unconsciously he had grasped her arm with the force of a vice.

But she did not speak again in that strain. She covered her face with her hands, and burst into a flood of tears,

"Dear Isabella, do me the favor to step into the next room a moment—I don't think there is any one there. I must reason with my sister a little. I know her troubles, you do not," cried Harry, at the same time leading her to the folding doors of the back room, which he opened.

But he was mistaken when he said there was no one there. Upon a sofa reclined a lady—one who looked as if she came from the land where cheeks are dark, and blood is warm. Her hair was black as the inner feathers of a raven's breast, her eyes large, dark as jet, and languishing too, as ever threw dangerous glances at a man. Her form was large, but faultless in proportion, and as she started to her feet at their entrance, she really looked beautiful. She had been reading, but she dropped the book upon the floor as she arose.

Harry quickly stepped across the room, and picked it up, saying,

"Ah! is it you, Miss Emma? Don't be alarmed, I pray you— I've a friend of my *sister's* here, whom I will leave with you a moment, for I wish to see *Maria*, alone!"

The girl looked at him with astonishment, but a glance from him, and a single whispered word of caution, and a promise of money acted like a charm. She at once seemed to understand the whole matter.

"Any friend of dear Maria, or of her good brother is welcome with me!"

"Then, Isabella, I'll leave you with Miss Wood a few moments—when sister is more calm, I'll call you in."

He returned to the front parlor, drew close the doors after him, and again stood by the side of Maria. She was still in tears; sobbing loudly.

"Maria, what does this mean? what has made you so chicken-hearted all at once?"

"Oh God! Harry Whitmore, I was once like *her*—spare her, for the love of Heaven. Can you look at her innocent face, and hear her pure thoughts, and still demon-like seek to destroy her?"

"Pshaw, girl, you don't think I'd destroy her—you're not destroyed—and I would'nt make her worse than you are!"

"No—you *couldn't!* And yet you would add one more crime to my fearful catalogue! Oh, Harry, if you are a man, give over this intention!"

"Maria Deloraine, you have known me three years now—have you ever heard that I backed from a design of this kind, when I had once made my mind up; or that I ever failed in it, when 'twas once begun?"

The girl only answered with a shudder. She knew that all he said was but too true. He continued:

"I will be kind and careful in this matter Maria, but it *must* be carried through. You have engaged in it, received pay, and promised to do as I wish!"

"Oh Heavens—too, too true! but Harry spare me."

"Maria, it is too late; but I will reward you better. When she is mine, you shall have one thousand dollars."

"One thousand dollars?" muttered the girl, who had ceased sobbing; "one thousand dollars? Often I have vowed, if ever I could get so much together, to go where I was unknown, and to commence a new life; to live once again virtuously."

"Well, Maria, now is your chance. You can make it."

"Yes, but at the expense of a human soul—at the expense of all which that poor girl possesses, that is worth living for. Oh, Harry, I *cannot!*"

"Cannot, girl! There is no such word for me. You shall have your choice. I will soon let Mrs. Windeman know what you are—I'll have your name *heralded* through the city, till you are as well known as Clara Norris, or any other of the stock company of the theatre of vice in the city. Choose, and that speedily! Shall it be the *thousand?*"

The poor girl shuddered, but she knew that she was at his mercy, and she feared the public exposure which he threatened. Beside this, *interest* was gnawing out the good feelings which had just began to grow in her heart, for a dream and hope, which she has long cherished, was now within her reach; she could, by a compliance with his wishes, gain the means of forever quitting the sickening life which she so long had led.

Her tears ceased. With a pale cheek, and a sad calmness

which was strong and firm, because forced with a desperate effort, she said :

"It shall be as you will. Yes, though it sinks my soul into hell itself, and tears the last good principle from my wretched heart—I will do it. Call in your victim. I'll wheedle and smile *now!* oh, yes, I'll be a very queen of deception!"

"Now you talk like a good sensible girl, as you are!" said Harry, quite contented to see the storm pass over, which had so nearly wrecked his designs.

He then went to the back-parlor door, and opening it, cried :

"You can come in now, dear Isabella. The shower is over, and the sun has come out!"

Isabella gladly obeyed his request, and when she saw a smile once more on Maria's face, her own brightened up, and she sprang into her arms, and kissed her sweetly.

"Oh, I am so happy, dear sister. May I not call you sister, Maria ?"

"Certainly, if you like to. My brother appears in a hurry to make you such."

The young girl blushed, while Harry caught her to his arms, pressed his lips warmly to hers, and said :

"Yes, dearest, our marriage shall not be long delayed. I cannot live so much from your side :—but 'tis getting late, I don't wish to hurry you, but I've an engagement to keep, which makes time precious to me. Beside, I've your brother to meet this evening, and some arrangements to make for him before then."

These "arrangements" were only to prepare Mr. Carlton and his gang for the meeting, which the reader already is aware of. But the sister little dreamed of this. She replied to his remark :

"Do urge him to come home earlier, dear Henry. He stays out so late, and often, that I fear he is hurting his health. He looks very pale, and care-worn lately."

"He has so much to do, dearest. The head book-keeper of such an establishment as that of S——, has a great deal of labor and much responsibility."

" Yes," replied the young girl, with a sigh, " I wish that I was rich, he should not toil so any longer."

" You will be, soon, dearest—but put on your bonnet and cloak, again. We must go."

This was done—a kiss and an invitation to call, was exchanged between the two girls, and then Isabella returned homewards.

CHAPTER VIII.

It was night—the night after that when Charles Meadows was so completely " done" by Carlton and his fiendish gang, and of course the first night for Angelina and her mother in their new quarters, in Laight street. The two were in a small but neatly furnished little parlor, or sitting-room. A small cooking-stove, with its pipe leading through into the chimney of the boarded-up fire-place, was nearly red-hot, and on its top a tea-kettle steamed up cheerily, singing as merrily as a "cricket on the hearth."

The open door of a little chamber on one side of them, showed the white counterpane and neat tester of a bed, one very unlike the little cot which had served them as a resting-place in the cellar, where they had *existed*, we can scarcely say, *lived*.

There was not much furniture. Livingston had hired this, and had not been very extravagant either, in his outlay, but still this was luxury, compared to the bare, cracked walls of their abode.

Angelina sat by the little pine work-table in one corner, sewing, as usual, but her good mother was engaged in setting her tea-table, and she made more bustle about it, than would ten servants in a fashionable house, for it had been very long since she was able to spread a cloth upon her table, and to put unbroken plates, cups, saucers, &c. upon it. And her comments too, as she set out the things, were really amusing, and even brought an occasional smile upon the thin face of her poor child.

"I do declare! I never!" she would cry, as she placed each new dish upon the table—"I never did set a table so nicely before in all my life. Things will taste so good, 'Lina, dear! Don't work any more to-night, child! Just get up, and look how nice I've got every thing laid!"

The girl did so, but as she looked at the table, she exclaimed in a tone of surprise:

12

"You've set the table for three, mother!"

"Yes, child. The kind gentleman said he'd be here to take tea with us!"

"Oh, mother, do not ask him here. Indeed he means some dreadful wrong. He would not be so generous to us if he did not expect some return."

"Tush! child. You are always so suspicious. Directly, you'll begin to think that *I'd* conspire to wrong you."

"Oh, no, dear mother!" cried the young girl, bursting into tears, and throwing her thin arms around her neck, "Do not say so, dear mother, I know you well, but I cannot drive from my brain, the memory of that dreadful night, and the connection which this man had with it."

"But, child, he has said that he drank too much wine on that night; that he did not know what he was doing. He certainly apologised very handsomely."

"Yes, mother, but—"

The young girl's reply was cut short, by a rap at the door, and while the mother hastened to open it, Angelina hurried into the bed-room, and closed the door.

"Ah, good evening, madam. Hope you're well, *very* well! where is your beautiful daughter, and how *is* she?" said Mr. Gus. Livington, in a free and easy manner, as he entered.

"Well—I do declare. Why, the child has gone and hid herself in the bed-room. She is *so* timid, sir; you must forgive her, for it is natural to the poor child. I was so once."

Livingston bit his lip with vexation, but took the chair which the old lady placed near the stove for him, and said:

"Your daughter has no occasion to fear me. I'm sure she never had a truer friend than myself."

"I know it, sir, indeed I do; but Angelina was so frightened on that first night, when you met her in Broadway, that she cannot get over it."

"I wish that *I* could get over that night!" said Livingston, and he sighed deeply.

"Why, sir," asked the mother, "was you harmed on that night?"

"Harmed, madam! if your daughter thus continues to hate and

fear me, indeed I was. I saw her then—have *loved* her ever since !"

" Oh, my gracious, me ! I thought so !" murmured the old lady, in an under tone, and with an expression of satisfaction on her thin face—the poor girl will marry a rich gentleman, and we wont have to work any more !"

Livingston either did not, or pretended not to hear this, and continued :

" It was this which led me to seek her out—to find where, and how you lived. It was this which has caused me to relieve you from your suffering condition, and it is this which will keep you ever in comfort !"

" Oh, my ! I thought as much ! If the poor girl was not so much afraid of you, I should be *so* happy !"

" She will soon get acquainted with me, and like me better. I don't think that I am so very frightful !"

" Oh, no, sir ; you are gentle, kind, and very good-looking. I will talk to her, and try to make her like you better."

" Do, my good woman, do ! Get her to come out and take tea, at least."

The mother went into the bed-rooom, and closed the door after her, while Gus. remained in his chair, carelessly whistling over an air, from some opera or other.

It was several minutes before the bed-room door opened again, and Gus. had heard loud whispering from the mother, and sobs from the daughter. But at last, the former seemed, in a measure, to have conquered the repugnance of the girl, for she came in leading her by the hand.

When Angelina entered, her face was pale as Parian marble ; her eyes red with weeping ; but when she met the burning glance of the libertine fixed upon her beautiful, though fast withering form, the poor girl's cheeks were in a moment covered with blushes. Her pure heart seemed instinctively to read his designs ; her nature caused her very soul to close against, and shrink from him, as doth the leaf of the sensative-plant, when touched by the rude hand of man.

He arose, and reaching out his hand, said, in a low and respectful tone :

"I had hoped that you would have forgiven my rudeness before now, Miss. Indeed, it makes me very unhappy to know that you are angry with me."

She did not take his hand, but in a faltering voice, replied:

"I am not angry with you, sir. I have forgiven you, I hope God has."

"Thank you, I shall feel more happy now, but not, if you ever treat me with so much coldness."

"It is better, sir," replied the young girl, in a firmer tone— "for you know how different are our situations. We never can be intimate, You are a gentleman, a rich one, I suppose. You know that I am a poor, uneducated sewing-girl."

"You need be so no longer. You are too delicate and beautiful for such a life."

"I shall not lead it long, sir!" replied the girl, in a sad tone, which told that thoughts of death were in her heart.

"Not a month longer; no, not a week, *dear* girl, without your wish!" said he passionately.

"Oh, mother! dear mother, do not leave me here alone!"

This exclamation was caused by the mother taking up the water pail, and going to the door, and Angelina was afraid to be left for a moment, in such company. But her mother, who thought her presence only a draw-back upon him, whom she wished to become her daughter's husband, made this an excuse for leaving them a moment together.

"I'm only going out to the pump, for a bucket of water. It is only a few steps from the door; I'll be back in a moment, child!" cried the mother, not even pausing at her child's request.

The moment she was gone, Livingston continued:

"Yes, dear girl; I love you, and will make you mine!"

"How?" and as the young creature asked that question, she fixed her clear blue eyes on his, with an expression which would read every thought in his heart.

He could not stand that look. His eye fell beneath it, and he blushed up to the very temples while he hesitated to answer.

She noted this, and exclaimed.

"I *knew* it was so! You have sought me, but to destroy me, as the hunter seeks his game!"

"Oh, no, dear girl, you wrong me! I did not understand your question!"

"Then hear it plainly. Would you marry me—would you link yourself to me by the laws of God and man?"

"Yes—that is, as soon as I can. I am so situated with my parents that—"

"Oh, sir, you need make no excuses. Your hesitation in answering me would be proof, if nothing else occurred, of your intentions. But did you really wish and intend to marry me, you *could* not."

"Could not? Why, my beautiful—oh, why?"

"Because, sir, *I do not love you.* No man living can ever claim my hand, who does not possess my heart; no, not were he possessed of uncounted gold, and I had to work the hand which I refused him, to the bare bones."

"Oh, do not speak so. You must—you *shall* be mine!"

"Never, sir, *never!*" replied the young girl, proudly and firmly. "If it is this that has caused your bounty to my poor mother, take it back. We can return to our cellar, we still can work, and earn enough to keep us alive."

"Foolish girl, you know not what you refuse. Beware how you push my love from you, for you can be made to feel that a slighted lover can become a bitter enemy."

"I care not, sir. My trust is in God! You cannot harm me, for He, the All-powerful, is my protector!"

"Girl, you seem determined to defy me. Do you not know that I can go to your employers, whom I know, and cut you off from work?"

"There are others who can employ me."

"Were I to go to these, and say you were no better than the girls who nightly walk the streets, would they employ you?"

"It would be false—cruelly false!" cried the poor creature, bursting into tears.

"Yet they would believe me quicker than you!"

"God would know the truth! oh, leave me, now, sir, if there is a spark of true manhood in you, leave me!" moaned the poor girl in her agony.

"You had better not force me too far. You never shall rest—

you cannot hide from me. I have offered to make you my wife —you have refused it, now you shall be—"

He whispered that last word in her ear, and it must have been one of horrible import, for she sprang from his side, and shrieked as if a serpent had stung her to the heart.

She rushed toward the street door. Another moment, and she would have been in the gloom and darkness without, had not the door opened, and her mother appeared.

"What is the matter, child? Dear Angelina, what is the matter?" cried the mother, terrified by her daughter's actions, and palid looks, and setting down her pail of water, she put her arms around the trembling creature, to keep her from falling.

"We must go from here, mother; we must leave this place!" sobbed the poor girl.

"Leave it, child? What does this mean? Has he dared to insult my poor girl."

"Oh, mother, ask no questions—but let us go!"

"What! not wait for tea, when it is all ready, and I've set out things so nice?"

"Wait for nothing, that comes from *his* hands, mother! It would be poison to our souls."

"Oh, what has he been doing—come into the bed-room, and tell me, child!"

"She need not leave my presence, to tell you, madam. I offered to make her my wife—she scornfully refused me, and then I said words in my haste, which I did not mean; words which I was sorry for the moment I uttered them. I hope she will forget them and forgive me."

"Never—never!" exclaimed the indignant girl, "and, sir, if you do not now, this instant, leave this room, I will! I would rather wander about exposed to all the dangers of the streets, than to live for one moment in a palace where you were present!"

"It shall be as you wish. I will come here no more!" replied the villain, in a tone of remorse. "My ardent, passionate nature carried me too far; a banishment from your presence will indeed be a punishment to me!"

After saying this, he took his hat, cane and cloak, bowed respectfully, and departed.

The moment he was gone, the sewing-girl, turned to her mother, and while the tears streamed down her cheeks, said:

"I am sorry for your sake mother, to leave all these comforts, but we must. I must hide from the dreadful persecutions of that man. He is indeed what I feared he was, and will do everything on earth now, to accomplish my ruin—in both body and soul!"

"Where can we go, child—where can we go? back to our miserable cellar?"

"No, mother, he would find us out there. There is one place where we can go—it is a dreadful spot, but we would be safer there, because he never would think I would choose such a place to live in!"

"Where is it, child?"

"It is down in a part of the city that is called the Five Points. When I worked for those clothing men in Chatham street, I went across through there, to go by a nearer way, one day, and I met a very poor woman, to whom I gave a shilling."

"Oh, yes, I remember that. You gave her a shilling when you had but four."

"I asked her where she lived," continued Angelina, "and she showed me a large house called the Brewery, where she said all the *very* poor people lived. It is a horrible place mother, but we can live there a little while, till this monster loses sight of me, or forgets me!"

"Oh, child, it is hard to leave all these good things, and to be poor again!" murmured the mother.

"Better far to do that, than to be unfitted both for earth and Heaven, mother! I can bear poverty, but not degradation."

"So can I, child. God forgive me for repining, but it was to save your health, that I was so unwilling to give up these comforts."

"We will do very well, mother—but we must go early, for he will have a watch kept over us, I fear, to see where we go!"

"I'll do just as you wish, child. You are my only comfort,

now your poor father has gone. I am glad that you got his ring back!"

"So am I, dear mother!" and as she spoke, Angelina kissed the large cornelian ring which she had upon her fore-finger. It was shaped like a shield, and had a coat of arms and crest engraven upon it.

CHAPTER IX.

AT the same hour, in a back room of the same house where occurred the last scene between Mary Sheffield, and Mr. Shirley, in our sixth chapter, two persons were seated side by side in conversation.

In the fine figure, high white brow, clear blue eyes, and fine features of the lady, the reader is permitted to recognise Mrs. Carlton, her whom we last saw comfortably quartered in the splendid suit of apartments above the gambling hell of Mr. Carlton.

The gentleman who was with her, was a middle-sized, rather well-formed person; had blue eyes, fair complexion, and light brown hair. His face had very little intellectuality in its expression, though the features were regular, and rather pleasing. He was a little over-dressed, that is, there was a rather unnatural pretension to fashion—which the true gentleman never assumes. Many of our readers may have noticed the almost professional look of a smart, showy stage-agent; or of an outside hotel-runner; or of some of our city merchant "drummers." If so, they will know precisely how this gentleman, Mr. Charles Cooly, looked.

He was seated very close to the lady, and held one of her small white hands in his, while he conversed with her.

"You say your husband is jealous?" said he.

"Yes," replied the lady, "he is, and cruelly so. But I am used to it now—he has ever been so, even since the day we were married. Had he not been jealous of me, when I was as constant to him as is an angel to its God, I never would have done as I have, and given him cause for jealousy."

"Does he suspect me?"

"No. He can place his suspicions on no one, because we have been so very cautious. He followed me once, I think, but I threw him off my track, by taking an up-town omnibus, and going so far up."

"Oh, yes; it was that cold blustering night—when I so feared you would catch cold."

"The same; when I called you out, and we took a brief walk together."

"Where is he now—if he should follow you to this house, he would at once know all!"

"I'm very cautious, dear Charles; for well I know his fearful temper. Should he catch us here at any time, both our lives would surely be the forfeit. Oh, I have passed through scenes with him, which I cannot describe."

"Why do you remain with him, then, dearest. Why do you not at once fly with me to the west, or somewhere that will place us beyond his reach?"

"Oh, Charles, my children, I cannot leave them! My darling little boy, and sweet daughter, how can I desert them? No, we will wait till something occurs that may make us more happy."

"It shall be as you wish, dearest. I only seek for your love and happiness. Were I rich, I would at once say, take them, and fly with me;—but, as it is, you know how I am struggling to get along. Had I more capital, I would go into some other business. I do not like the one I am in at present."

"It is better than that which my husband follows. If it is less profitable, still it is more creditable."

"True," replied Cooly, " but it is not one which suits my feelings."

"You will have another, I hope, soon. Whenever you want money, come to me. I can always command some!"

"Oh, I thank you, dear Hannah, but I will not call upon you for funds. Your *love* is all that I ask."

"That you have, Charles. I think you have had proof enough of that."

"I have, indeed, Hannah, but such proofs are ever welcome to me," and as he spoke, the man bent forward and impressed a long, passionate kiss upon her voluptuous lips.

She returned it with fervor—threw her arms around his neck,

and—we will leave this scene for another. It will not be proper for us to stay here longer.

———

On the morning succeeding the night, when Charles Meadows had fallen back senseless, after his attempt at suicide, after a broken and nervous slumber of perchance an hour or two, the unhappy young man awoke. Mr. Carlton was by his side—Harry Whitmore had left.

The eyes of Meadows opened, but he closed them again with a shudder.

A cold sneering smile passed over the face of the gambler—a smile more expressive of his cold-blooded, fiendish nature, than we can find words to describe.

"How are you this morning, my young friend?" asked he.

Again Charles opened his eyes, then pressed his hands to his forehead convulsively, while in a faint tone, he murmured:

"I've had a horrible dream!"

"A dream, indeed!" said Carlton, "you've been very sick."

"Yes—where am I? This is not home! in the prison already?" and as he spoke, the young man gazed wildly around him.

"Ha! ha! That *is* an idea!" laughed Carlton. "This looks like a prison, don't it. 'Tis the best furnished one in all America, if it is!"

The scattered senses of the young man began to be more collected—he looked upon the rich furniture of the apartment, and felt that his body was stretched upon a yielding bed of down. Recognizing him who stood by the bed-side, he spoke:

"Am I yet in your house, Mr. Carlton?"

"You are, sir, and I have watched by you all night, or at least, all the morning. It was nearly three when you were taken sick."

"Sick?" murmured the wretched youth, "have I been sick? I feel as if I had been dreaming of some strange and horrible scene."

"You were crazy as a loon. Do you remember trying to kill yourself? Nothing but a bad percussion cap saved you.

It's a good thing to have caps that will explode, sometimes, but at *others*, as in this case, a bad one saves a deal of trouble."

"I don't know what you are talking about!" replied Charles; his senses evidently still wandering.

"Then just listen to me. You remember losing your money in fair play, at my table?"

"Yes; my dear friend Harry was there."

"That is true. Do you remember what you did, after leaving the table?"

"No; I must have drank too much."

"You were not drunk, but you were desperate. You tried to blow out your own brains, but the pistol didn't go off; so you *did*—into a fainting fit."

"Now I know all. You had me brought here instead of sending me home. I thank you for the forethought. It has saved my mother and sister's feelings. I thank you, indeed I do."

"Never mind thanks, sir, I have other things to talk with you about. I know the cause of your desperation."

"The *cause*, sir? What do you mean—have I been talking in my delirium?"

"It matters not how *I* found it out, but old S—— would be rather wrathy if he knew of those odd thousands, eh?"

With a convulsive bound, even as if he had been shot through the heart, Meadows sprang from the bed, and while with a palid face and glaring eyes he confronted Carlton, he almost shouted:

"For God's sake, tell me how you knew this!"

"It matters not," replied Carlton, "how I came by it, so that I know it."

"Well, sir, what will you do—expose me?" The young man spoke in a thick and husky tone, which told his perfect desperation.

Carlton paused a moment before he answered, as if it was a delight to him to torture the unfortunate clerk, and then replied:

"No—not if you treat me right."

"Treat you right? Must I *bribe* you to silence."

"You needn't use that *word* for it, but as you are in my power, you must not hesitate to accede to my wishes."

"*Must* not? Henry Carlton you are talking to a desperate

man. . By heaven if you do not swear before God, this moment, to keep this terrible secret, I'll shoot you as I would a dog."

"Shoot away; I will *not* swear!" replied the gambler, with his habitual cold and fiendish sneer.

The young man's hand was thrust quick as thought, into the side pocket, whence he had drawn his pistol on the preceding evening, but the weapon was not there. It had been taken care of.

Carlton saw his look of disappointment, and while he laughed, he cried :

"I always keep dangerous play-things out of children's hands. Now will you come to terms ?"

"What terms? I have no money. You took all I had in the game last night."

"You can get more, as you have already."

"Oh, God, no! I have already taken, and lost seventeen thousand dollars. I fear every hour to be found out."

"Oh, pshaw! You can run on a year in this way, while you keep the books and cash account yourself," replied the gambler, carelessly.

"And then, what! At the end of that year would come disgrace—a public trial—a states-prison, and—it would be death to my poor mother and sister !"

"Oh, no—no danger of that! There are very few people who die of disgrace—but in this case there's no need of any one knowing it."

"How can it be helped? Tell me, in God's name, tell me !"

"If you'll do as I wish you to, I'll see that you are never found out, and show how to make an odd fifty thousand for yourself."

"How? Explain, if you care for my misery at all, explain !" groaned Meadows.

The gambler fixed his keen eye upon him, and continued.

"You know how large a stock old S—— keeps, and how much cash he has on hand ?"

"Yes, very nearly. He never has less than from four to five hundred thousand dollars worth of goods on hand, but he deposits most of his money in bank.   We seldom have more than four or five thousand dollars in cash in at once."

"That's only pin-money.   Did you ever try your hand in forging?"

"No ; do not try to set me on another crime.   I have done too much already."

"Oh, pshaw ! You're too chicken-hearted. You're in for more than you can ever get again, why not make a haul worth having.   The principle is the same.   If you're found out with what you have now done, you'll suffer just as much as if it was ten times more."

"True; too true.   I am in your power, now—what would you have me do ?"

"Only to draw a check at the *right* time, for all that you can get out of bank, in S——'s name.   On the night of the same day, through you, a gang of excellent fellows, Jack Circle's burglars, shall borrow the keys of you, or else get their own screws fitted, and 'lift' a few thousand dollars worth of silks and laces. Nothing more !"

"Nothing *more* !" echoed the unhappy clerk, " nothing **more** than to rob and completely ruin a man who has ever been my friend and benefactor."

"Why did you commence on him ?"

"Why—*why?*   Because one of your villainous, fiendish gamblers first led me on to play with my own funds.   Let me win till I was crazy with success, and then beat me.   I *borrowed* of my employer, unknown to him, till borrowing became stealing ; and here I stand a *thief !*"

"Well—well !   You use too many hard words, my boy, but as you abuse yourself as well as us, I don't know that I've any right to complain !   But we'll drop all this—I shall now consider you a partner of mine—if there is any sudden danger of your being found out in what you have taken, come to me, and I'll let you have the cash to get you out of it.   We must hold back, and make a large haul."

The young man answered not, but seated himself on the side of the bed, and seemed lost in thought.

Carlton regarded him a moment with evident satisfaction, and then said :

"Breakfast will be ready in ten or fifteen minutes in the next room, I'll leave you till then, to think over this matter. Only Sam Selden will breakfast with us, and he is one of *us*, you know."

Carlton left the room after making this observation, and Meadows was alone in his *misery.*

CHAPTER X.

JACK CIRCLE and Genlis, he who styled himself the Gipsey fortune-teller, were alone in the upper back room of Jack's crib. A single candle dimly lighted the gloomy place, and gave the singular faces of these two men a dark and shadowy look. Genlis, was naturally very dark, especially about the upper part of his face, which was much shaded by his heavy black hair. He seemed to be concocting some plan with old Jack, for he shook his head at some proposition made by the latter, and said in his usual low, deep tone :

"It wont do, Jack! It wont do—the coppers are too wide awake!"

"They does keep their peeps purty vide hopen; it's a fact, but wool can be hauled over 'em for all that!" replied Jack, who seemed bent on having some plan of his adopted.

"It is true—but we want to make one or two large hauls ; lifts that will make folks stare more than they ever have on this side of the big fish-pond. I don't like to run any risk for small things—I'd peril life and everything for a large chance."

"So 'd I," responded Jack, "but we must keep a goin, if it's only to keep the boys' hands in."

"We've too many in the clan—it is very unsafe to trust our secrets to so large a crowd."

"No—it's not unsafe, 'cause these fellers all knows me, and if I thought one of 'em would peach I'd do him so!"

Here Jack drew his fore-finger very significantly across his throat, and added : "I've seen more 'an one feller sarved in that ere vay!"

Genlis now took out his watch, and after noting the hour, asked :

"What time did Tobin say he would be here?"

"Vy, he was to be here habout ten—it arn't more than that now, is it ?"

"Yes, ten minutes over. I'd like to see him—he is a keen boy, in his own way.

"Yes, but it's in sich a werry small line. I does like to see men hambitious in everythin', 'specially in our line."

What the response of Genlis would have been, we do not know, but a rap at the door, in the usual significant way, announced an intruder.

"Who's there ?" asked Jack, gruffly.

"One frent, and his companie !" replied the person without, his tone and broken English at once announcing him as the French Captain.

"Ah, is that you, uncle Tommy ?" and as he said this, Jack hastened to open the door.

"Yes, sare, all zat is left of me in zis dam bad wezzare !—ze dam rheumatiz, it most kill me several times !" and as he said this, Captain Tobin came in, followed by a person closely muffled in a large cloak, with a common cap drawn down so much over his eyes, as nearly to conceal his face.

"Who the devil 'ave you got there, as seems afeard to show his phiz 'mongst honest folks like us ?" asked Circle, looking very hard at the pick-pocket's companion.

The reply was given by the stranger casting off his cloak.

"Ah, is it you, Carlton ?" cried Genlis, and then while he warmly shook his hand, he added, "how goes things on at the bank ?"

"Swimmingly ! plenty to do, and all of the boys at work." Then, turning to Jack, the gambler said:

"I've come to put up a job for you and your gang, Jack !"

"Vel, vot is it ?—Ve're allers on 'and for anythin' as 'll pay."

"This will—to a big figure too, if you do it up right

"Vell, can't you tell a feller vot it is—and not keep him in hexpense all this ere time."

"You know old S——'s store ?"

"Him as keeps down there in Broadway, you means, doesn't you ?"

"Yes, the same."

" Yes I knows he's got an almighty lot o' stuff in his crib, and he must 'ave plenty of the dust too !"

" Well, I want that crib cracked."

" There's many a *vant* as is a *can't*, old feller ! why the coppers is paid to keep a 'special look out for that ere place. I'd as lives try to crack a Wall-street bank, right in the face of the private watchees and all."

" But I've got things fixed better than you know. I've some one that will fit your keys, and fix everything to your hand."

" Vot, a hinsider ?"

" Yes, one of his own clerks."

" Vel, then there's some sense in considerin' over the matter. Don't you think so, chums ?"

This last question was addressed to Tobin and Genlis.

The latter replied, that Harry Carlton knew what he was about, and that what he said was right, *was* right ; while Captain Tobin put his finger to one side of his nose, contracted his brow, paused apparenly for a moment's thought, and then replied :

" Yes, sare. I sink it will be von ver' grand speculatione !"

" We can make a swag of at least a couple of hundred thou sand, if it is done up right !" said old Jack, and then he added— " You just put it up your hone vay, Mr. Carlton, and when you wants the boys, just let me know, and they shall be on 'and with the tools."

" Well, that is understood ; now, what about that other affair of yours, Genlis, the one you was telling me of last evening ?"

" It will be all right. Inez is on the look out, and at the very first opportunity will seize the child."

" You'll make a grand spec out of that, I expect !"

" Well, I hope so—money is scarce with me now-adays."

" And yet business is not dull."

" No," replied the fortune-teller, " but then it is very trifling. Nothing but romantic young girls—clerks who sell tape and needles—Irish servant girls, &c. One can never make a fortune out of them, in fact, hardly a genteel living."

" Well, if you all work your cards right in the case you told me, and then get two or three more of the same kind, you'll pay up for lost time."

"It is true," replied Genlis, "and I don't think we can fail in this case."

A rap at the door, announced another visitor. As the right sign had been given, Jack Circle at once opened the door, and Frank Hennock entered.

"Hallo, youngster, vot is in the vind, now? Vot 'ave you come to report?"

"I came to see if Mr. Tarhound is here, I want to get him a good fat fee out of my new master."

"A fee! For what?" exclaimed Carlton.

"Only some of that infernal Hunt business! My head is racked all to pieces with it—and it really needs a lawyer to get his money."

"Then *get* a *lawyer*, don't get him. He's only fit to help thieves out of a dirty scrape," exclaimed Carlton, again, "he has no influence in court."

"But this is not a court business; it is only to draw up some *papers* that he is wanted. Beside I'm too well known to the lawyers generally, and this fellow depends so much on us that he'll be sure to keep silent."

"That's true; and silence is necessary."

"Vel, if you vants him, youngster, I'll see that he calls on your gov'nor!" said old Circle. "And now boys let's drink. I'm as dry as a fish out o' water. Frank, just tell 'Arriet to come up ven you goes down, ve are habout to tipple. And you may tell her to mix you summat warm, 'cause it must be cold out to-night."

Frank at once took the hint to leave, and in a few moments the old man's daughter came up. As she thrust her face into the half-opened door, leaving her body outside, she asked:

"What'll it be my covies? Heavy wet? Cold or warm?"

"For me, brandy and water, cold," said Genlis.

"Ditto," added Carlton.

"What'll you have, old rheumatiz?" asked the woman, looking at Captain Tobin, who had quietly seated himself in a corner, and lighted a cigar.

"I shall 'ave some sing ver warm, madam; some sing zat

will make zis dam rheumatiz in ze back of my head, and my shouldares, go ver far away !"

"Rum toddy, a little cayenne in it, eh ?"

"Yes, I sink it shall be some room toddee !"

"What'll it be for you, dad ?" continued the girl.

"Rum, old *Jamake*, of course, hot as thunder, and sweet as you ar my gal !" replied old Circle, and the attentive daughter hurried away to *fill* her orders.

We will leave these men, and even let the night slip on without any further records of them.

———

It was the afternoon of another day. In her little basement, front sitting-room, sat Mrs. Annie Abingdon. Her little child was playing at her feet with a large assortment of toys, doubtless supplied by his fond father, who was not in sight. The mother was engaged in some needle-work, and as she stitched away, she hummed over a favorite song. Indeed that beautiful woman looked to be the very picture of happiness and contentment. Suddenly the child paused in his play, and seemed to listen with deep interest for a moment, to a sound which came faintly to his ear. At first, it was like the distant rumbling of carriages, then as it seemed to grow louder and louder, the child arose from the floor and ran across the room to the front door, where he again paused and listened. The sounds became more plain—the face of the little fellow brightened up, and a flash of pleasure illuminated it.

"Oh, ma, *dear* ma," he cried—"the soldiers are coming. Oh, hear the drums ! Do let me go to the door !"—and now the full burst of music from a brass band came sweeping through the air.

As the little fellow spoke, he raised on his tip-toes and managed to open the door. His mother had hardly raised her eyes from her work, but as she heard the spring of the latch, she cried:

"Don't go out, my dear. 'Tis too cold for you."

"Only to the door, ma, to see the soldiers !" said the child, and ere she could answer, he had gone out to the steps which fronted the house.

As he stood here, he saw the gay uniforms, flaunting banner and burnished weapons of a company of city volunteers, and then as they came up, his eye fell upon the crowd of children who were rushing along to see the soldiers. He was completely carried away with the music and the glitter, and almost unknowingly, he straggled on with the rest. He had not gone very far, when a kind-looking lady spoke to him.

"Whose boy are you, my child?" she asked in kind tones.

"I'm Willie Abingdon," said the little fellow, while he looked up at her with a mingled look of curiosity and fear at being spoken to by a stranger.

But her smile was very kind, and when she took him by the hand and led him into a confectionary near by, and bought him some candies, his conquest was made, and he really for the moment forgot his mother. It is true that this lady who was so kind to him, had dark eyes, hair and skin, all of these very unlike his mother's, yet she like the latter had a soft voice, and a very kind tone.

After she had supplied him with candies, and given him a very pretty little sugar horse, the lady took him by the hand, and led him out into the street. The soldiers were gone—the crowd had passed on. The little boy could hear the distant sound of the receding music—but his thoughts were now of home—he wished to hurry there, to show his mother his pretty presents. A carriage stood in front of the door, a very handsome carriage, with two large fine-looking horses attached to it.

"Oh, what pretty horses!" cried the boy, clapping his little hands together with pleasure as he looked upon them.

"Do you think so, my 'child? Does not the carriage look pretty too?" asked the lady.

"Oh, yes ma'am, it is very pretty. Oh, how I'd like my ma to have one like it!"

"Would you? Dont you want to take this to her?"

"Oh yes, ma'am, if it was mine, I would! Is it yours?"

"Yes, child! Do you want to ride in it?"

"I'd like to, ma'am, but I can't. I must go home," replied the boy, with a manner which showed that the ride would indeed be a pleasure to him.

The lady noted this, and her dark eyes gleamed strangely bright, as she saw it.

"Come with me, and ride home in the carriage, my little pet!" said she.

The boy did not hesitate—he let her lift him into the carriage, and as the driver closed up the steps, she cried—"Home first—to the boat next! Be quick!"

The driver mounted his box and drove rapidly off, while the woman, INEZ GENLIS, clasped the beautiful, stolen child in her arms.

At the very moment when that carriage, with its closed pannels, and drawn curtains, passed the door of the Abingdons, that poor child's mother was standing on the door-step, looking up and down the street for her child. That child was within the reach of her voice, and yet she knew it not. She had not missed him until the sound of the music and marching-men had gone by, and then she thought that he might have gone up stairs, or back into the kitchen.

Running back to the latter, she called to Katrine, her Dutch servant girl:

"Katrine, is Willie with you?"

"No, ma'am! He ish not pe here since I wash clear up de taple!"

"Oh, Heaven! What can have become of him; run up stairs, look in every room for him! I'm so afraid he has got off into the street, and will be lost."

The servant hurried up stairs, and again the mother went to the front door, and strained her eyes up and down the street, looking for her lost one. But it was in vain. She rushed back into the sitting-room, only in time to meet the servant, who could not find the child up stairs.

"Oh, Merciful Heaven! he must be lost!" moaned the mother, in agony—"run Katrine—run down the street, and ask everybody you meet. I'll go up—Oh, what shall I do! what will Edward say!"

With her cheeks pale from terror—her eyes streaming

with tears, the mother snatched up her hood, and without waiting for her shawl, rushed out in search of her child. The servant also went out, and as they did so, forgot in their hurry even to shut the door.

Twenty minutes later, Edward Abingdon returned from down town, in an omnibus. As he reached his door, he was astonished to see it left standing open on a day so cold, and more surprized when he found the sitting-room entirely deserted. The man-servant was not there—he called for Katrine, and she too was absent. He did not know but his wife might have taken the child, and gone into a neighbor's house for a few moment's visit, but at the moment when this thought struck him, he saw the little fellow's cap and cloak; and he knew that his Annie was too careful of her babe, to take it out in such severe weather, without being well wrapped-up.

He hurried up stairs—went into every apartment and called upon the names of his wife and child. But his only answer came from the echoing walls.

He hurried down stairs again, for he began really to be frightened, and he had more reason to be when he met his wife who was just staggering in through the door, as he re-entered the sitting-room.

"Oh, Edward—our child!" she screamed, and fell forward fainting in his arms.

"Annie, dear Annie, speak; tell me what is the matter!" cried the husband; but he spoke to one as senseless as a marble statue.

He hastily laid her down upon the sofa, and poured water freely over her face. He kissed her again and again, and tried every means to bring her to. But it seemed impossible. He however poured some of the water in between her lips, and then she showed some signs of returning consciousness. Her eye-lids began to quiver—next, her lips slightly opened, and a feeble sigh was breathed.

The husband renewed his exertions, and soon her eyes opened upon him.

"Oh, Heaven! Dear Edward, our poor child!" she murmured.

"What of it, Annie?   Where is he?"

"Oh, I cannot tell—I have looked every where, Edward The last I saw he stood in the door way, to see some soldiers who were passing.   In a moment he was gone from my sight— oh, God, I fear he is *lost!*"

A flood of tears came now to relieve her heavy heart, and while her husband raised her head to his bosom, he said:

"Do not feel so bad, dear Annie.   The child may have wandered away, but he will surely be found.   I will advertise for him, and send out searchers."

"God in mercy grant he may be found!" murmured the mother —"why has not Katrine returned?"

"Is she out looking for Willie?"

"Yes; I sent her one way, and went the other myself.   Oh, Edward, what shall we do if he is lost?"

"Trust to God, and use every exertion to find him, my love. It will do no good to despair!"

"It is true, Edward.   I will try to be more womanly.   Oh, how truly you spoke when you said that sorrow might come, and that it is best ever to be prepared for it."

At this moment Katrine returned, of course, without any knowledge of the child.   Leaving his wife in the care of Katrine, Abingdon hurried out to adopt measures for a search.   Although he had been more calm than his wife, he had as deeply felt the loss; but for her sake he had restrained and concealed his fear and anxiety.

CHAPTER XI.

"WELL, Gus., how are you this evening? Up for fun? Anything on hand, eh?" cried Harry Whitmore, not more than an hour after the last scene between Gus. and Angelina, had occurred. The two met just in front of the *Cafe des mille Colonnes.*

The brow of Livingston was contracted, and his voice stern and gruff, when he answered:

"No! I've been fairly bluffed off by that little stuck up thing, the sewing girl!"

"What! driven off the track, entirely? you don't mean it, Gus.!"

"I do mean that she has bluffed me off, but as to my leaving the track, that's another thing. By foul means if I can't use fair, I'll have her yet!"

"Well, go ahead, old boy; but you don't use the right means, my lad. Do things as smoothly as I do—you are too rough. A woman must be coaxed—you can't drive her half as easy as you can a mule."

"I tried coaxing," replied Livingston—"I took her and her mother from a cellar, where they were living poorer than church mice, and furnished two rooms for them, and paid the rent in advance."

"Well, that was all right, but did you at once go to making love?"

"Yes, I couldn't help it. That girl has driven me mad!"

"I should think so, by your actions. You ought to have been the disinterested benefactor, for at least a week or ten days. In that time, you might have won her confidence enough to have got her to ride out with you, then your way would be easy enough!"

"How?"

"Why, to have driven her to Leonard street, or down to Madame I.'s, to call on a *friend*.   Once inside the door, she never could help herself!"

"That's true, Harry. You have a natural talent for these things, which I can't acquire. Don't you think of any way that I can work now, to get hold of her?"

"Yes, a dozen!"

"Name one and the best, 'an thou lovest me Hal!' I should have advised with you at first!"

"Of *course* you should. But for her—let me see. Do you think she knows anything about the Leonard street dens?"

"No, I don't believe that she has any true knowledge of these places, or the people that live there.   She is verdant upon nearly all subjects—"

"Except that which she bluffed you off on!" said Harry, laughingly interrupting him.

"She is particularly verdant on that, or she would prefer my offers to the life of toil and suffering which she endures.   But, that plan of yours, Harry.   Let me hear it!"

"Just let Jule, or one of her girls send and hire the girl to come to the house to sew. When you get her in there, make her your own!"

"But she and the old woman will raise the devil with me. They'll make a fuss, and get Matsell, or some other keen-eyed magistrate on my track, and then will come a trial, which of course will be *heralded* to the world if I don't lay down black mail enough to buy twenty black females at the Orleans price."

"No. You needn't fear that. The girl when once ruined, would keep silent for her own sake. You'd have every thing your own way, when you had completed your designs."

"By Jove, I believe I would! Give me you for a planner, yet, Harry.

"I'm full as good in executing as I am in planning!"

"That is true ; and by the way what puts you into such good spirits ?"

"Nothing more than that I've been as lucky as you have unfortunate."

"What! You don't mean to say that you have succeeded already in that Meadows case?"

"No, not exactly succeeded, but l have everything sure. I do these things more calmly and deliberately, but far more certainly than you. I follow the tactics of Aaron Burr!"

"I should say you did; especially in your deliberation and perseverance. I've heard old men say that Burr never laid his eye upon a woman whom he was pleased with, that escaped his snare!"

"That is true; nor have I. But let's go in out of this, and take a *smile*. It is too cold to stand here talking."

As the two went into Pinteux, Harry continued:

"Which way were you bending, Gus., when we met?"

"I was going up town to meet Bill Lord, Butcher Bill, Ned Shorter, and some others of *the* boys, to have a round. I was mad and intended to get these fellows out on a bender, and then to raise a muss somewhere. I'd like to see a fight to-night—I would, by thunder!"

"Well don't let me be any draw-back to your laudible intentions or pat-riot-ick wishes."

"Ah, Harry, you're a wag, always punning. Who said anything about raising an Irish row. I'd rather see those boys in at Pete's on the Points, than anywhere else. 'Twould do you good to see them knock the darkies round. Niggers stand an almighty sight of beating, you know!"

"Yes, if you don't hit them on the shins—but what'll you imbibe? The lady behind the bar is waiting."

"Punch—old Monongehela, hot!" replied Livingston, at the same time smiling most benignly upon the bar-maid, who of course returned it, for she smiled on all customers.

The beverage was mixed, a ditto was done for Harry, and soon they disappeared where many of their spiritual relatives had gone before.

"Where are you bound to?" asked Gus. in turn of Harry, as the latter drew on his right hand glove after paying for the liquor.

"Well, I *was* about to drop down to Carlton's to see if any of the boys were there; or in at Jack Harris' to pass off an hour or two—but if you feel like taking a round, I'll go along, I've nothing particular on hand."

"Where's Charley Meadows, to-night?"

"He's sick; he hasn't got over that Carlton scene, yet. I suppose he'll be all straight though, before long."

The two now left the bar-room, and we will answer to the reader that last question of Livingston's. Where is Charles Meadows?

At the very hour when they were speaking of him, the unhappy young man was seated before his writing desk in his little chamber at home. His face was pale—his whole appearance ghastly. A partly finished letter lay before him—he had paused and seemed to be trying to settle his mind down upon some dark and desperate thought. He had crushed the quill pen, with which he had written, between his teeth, and had unconsciously drawn his sleeve over a part of his writing, and made it but an illegible blot.

Taking the spoiled pen from his lips, and dashing it upon the floor, he arose and commenced pacing the room. As he did so, his thoughts were expressed in audible soliloquy.

"It must be. I am dishonored enough now—I had better die than plunge myself deeper into crime! Yes; one touch, one instant can end my present misery but—" and that young man trembled as he spoke—"there is a *future*! Oh, God, to me earth is now a hell; if I die there is but another hell waiting for me! Oh, misery! *misery!*"

He paused and looked around the room. Upon his toilet table lay many a neat little article made by his young sister's hand-the room had been arranged by her. On his reading table lay a bible presented by his fond mother. But too seldom had he opened its leaves. While he looked upon these, the thoughts of his contemplated suicide came up again.

"Oh, God! Can I leave them?" he murmured—"and yet rather than live to see them suffering from my disgrace I would die a thousand deaths. I cannot, will not survive it—and it must be found out. The books may be examined in my absence —yes, by the Heaven whose laws I am about to break, *I will do it!*"

He stepped hastily across the room, and opened a small dressing case. From beneath a paper in its bottom, he took a phial and as he held it up between him and the light, his wild eye read in large letters on the label,

"BE CAREFUL—PRUSSIC ACID."

"Careful!" said he, and he laughed wildly—"very great cause have I to be careful. A few moments more, and care will be all over for me!"

That young man was calm now, even as if he had been about to take a glass of wine, or some pleasant cordial. His face was deathly pale, his lips blue and cold, his eyes dilated, but brilliant, more so even than when we have seen him under the terrible excitement of the gaming table.

He walked to the table, took up another pen, and wrote a few more lines in the letter which lay there.

"There is no need of a seal or direction there," he said, "they will learn all, but too soon."

Then he arose, took the deadly phial in his hand, and went to the bed-side. He laid himself calmly down, uncorked the phial, and raised it to his lip.

Oh, why did he tremble then—pause in the fearful act, and spring from the bed!

He heard his sister's voice, cheerfully singing as she came up the stairs. The next instant he laid down the phial on the mantel-piece, for her hand was on the door latch, and her sweet voice paused in its song to ask:

"May I come in, dear brother?"

"Yes, Isabella!" said he hoarsely, "come in. I was about to *retire*, but you can come!"

She opened the door, but as she looked at his ghastly face, she cried:

"Oh, my poor brother—you are worse, you are very sick! Do let me send for the doctor! I must call mother!"

"No, Isabella, stay," replied he,—"I am a little unwell, but it is only a headache. I soon will recover from it.

"Oh, dear brother, I fear not. You don't know how sick you look!"

"No matter how I *look*, sister. Let me judge my health from my feelings. You may go and make me a cup of tea, if you will!"

"Yes, dear Charles, anything to do you good. You have toiled so hard, dear brother, lately, but you shall not do so much longer."

"No, I do not *intend* to!" said he with an emphasis which of course she could not understand. She hurried away to make his tea, and once more he was alone.

Again he took up the poison. He regarded it a moment steadily—then dashed it into the ash-pan beneath the coal-grate.

"I cannot leave her and my mother!" he said. "I will do this last villainy for Carlton, and raise funds enough to leave this land for ever, and to take them with me, where they cannot hear of my conduct. I will *hope* on, and not let despair again drive me to this pitch of madness."

CHAPTER XII.

MIDNIGHT had gone by, and the small hours of the morning were beginning to increase. Within the room where Mr. Precise found occasion to admire the wonderful agility of Pete Williams' Juba dancers, one of that colored gentleman's most fashionable hops was going on. The steam was up, and rich sounds, sights, and smells hailed the ears, eyes, &c., of all who entered. The colored *ladies* had thrown aside their neckerchiefs; the men had pitched off their over-coats and jackets, and the whole party, at least as many as could get on the floor at once, were laying down "their biggest licks."

The old fiddler and guitar-player were doing their best to make a noise, not being very particular as to harmony, or whether their instruments were in tune or not. Pete was behind the bar, aiding his regular bar-keeper in serving out the gin which his customers so frequently called for, and his grin was unusually wide and bright, for the change came in rapidly.

Green-eyed Andy was doing a capital business in the back room with some sailors, who, just from a cruise at sea, were having a cruise and spree on shore, to get rid of the extra cash which they had toiled three years for in Uncle Sam's service. Andy would once in a while let one of them win a quarter, but where one of them *won*, five others were sure to lose, so that he was doing a very safe business.

It was nearly three o'clock, and suddenly a noise was heard at the door, as if some altercation was taking place between the door-keeper and persons without. The next instant, the tall door-keeper was seen coming into the room head first like an arrow, pitching out as straight upon the flat of his back, as if he had been killed, while a fountain of blood gushed up from his mouth and nose.

"Clear the kitchen here! the white folks *are* a comin'!" cried a man who followed close upon the heels of the poor black, and who was himself followed by five others, among whom were our friends, Harry Whitmore and Gus. Livingston.

The first speaker was a man of medium height, but very thick-set, and powerfully-formed. He had rather a small head, but a thick, regular "bull-neck," and looked as if there was more of the bull-dog in his disposition, than there was of the man. As soon as he and his party got in, he folded his arms and looked over the whole of the assembly which had now stopped dancing.

"Go on with your music! keep up that dance, you black devils, you!" shouted the man whom we have just described. The musicians hesitated.

"Just keep the door, let nobody in or out there boys," said the first speaker, and then, with a hasty step, he crossed the room and ascended the little stand where the musicians were seated.

"Now *will* you oblige me, or shall I oblige you—you angels of hell!" said he, as he, caught each of them by an ear and cracked their two heads together.

"For God's sake, stop, Massa Bill! de lor ab marcy on de man as make you mad! We'll play!" cried the old fiddler, and as soon as the man let go, the music struck up.

"Now dance! Heave ahead there with your sets, or I'll be down on you, you soot-bags of mortality!" shouted the man, "you know *me*, the most of you, and if any of you don't, I'm Butcher Bill, gentleman, scholar, *and* so forth; professor of fist-ology, the black art, *and* so forth!"

The negroes seemed not only to know, but to fear him, for they obeyed his orders, and the dance went on.

Bill now descended from the stand, and walked over to the bar, where Pete stood half angry and half frightened.

"Give me some grog, nigger! Grog for me and my friends! Come here, boys, all of you but Dutch Charley, he is man enough to keep that door till I drink, and go and relieve him!" cried Bill, as he faced the bar.

The party, consisting of Harry, Gus., and two others, beside the one they called Dutch Charley, came up, and Pete, though looking as black as a thunder-cloud, handed down a decanter of brandy, and placed the tumblers before them.

Bill took up the decanter, smelt of the brandy, and then very quietly poured out a tumbler full of it, and pitched it in Pete's face; at the same time, saying:

"Is that the kind of stuff you set before gentlemen, you infernal Arab! Out with that black bottle which you keep for your own use!"

"My God, Massa Bill, dis is too much!" cried Pete, wiping the brandy from his eyes; "you nebber comes in here without raising up a rumpus!"

But Pete set out the black bottle, and Bill poured out a stiff horn therefrom for each of his friends. After they had drank, Bill poured out a glass for his friend at the door, and carried it to him. When this was done, he called his party together, and said in a lower tone than before—

"We'll have some fun now, boys. Yes, *we* will! Charley, you and Bill Lord stand by the door and don't let a nigger in or out, for love or money! Yes, Harry, Ned Shorter, Gus, and me will have a *cow-tillion*; yes, *we* will! Stop that music, for one minute, exactly!"

The music ceased—and Bill, walking into the centre of the room with his three friends, said:

"Now step out here 'yaller gals—the four prettiest and the best dancers! Be quick before I come and fetch you!"

Though at least a hundred dark-skinned females were present, they seemed to be all struck with a perfect unconsciousness of their personal charms. Not one seemed inclined to take upon herself the honor of being the best dancer and prettiest yellow girl in the room.

The brow of the bully (we beg his pardon, but it is useless to call an onion a rose,) began to darken again.

"Shall I come and pick you out, *ladies?*" cried he.

At last his appeal seemed to have some effect; a hideous, one-eyed, poc-marked, ragged girl, who looked as if she had been brought up scullion to his satanic majesty, stepped out and said:

"If dey is all afeared to dance wid you massa, I isn't. I hab de honor to answer to your call!" and she made such a curtsy as would have graced a sick elephant.

"Why, you blear-eyed, haggle-toothed, mud-colored devil!

14

What do you mean?   Are you the prettiest gal in this room?"
shouted Bill, making a step toward her, demonstrative of an intention to demolish her.

But she stood her ground and smiling horribly, said:

"Purty is as purty does, sah!   Dem's my senterments."

"So they're mine, too.   By thunder, you shall dance in this
set.   Here Gus., lead out this lady for your partner."

Livingston quietly put on his thick gloves, and did as he was
told, saying that he was in for his share of the fun whatever it
was.

Bill would not wait any longer to *invite* partners for the dance,
but walked directly up to the corner where the women had
huddled together, he seized one and giving her a shove into the
centre of the room, shouted:

"There she goes!   Look out for her, Whitmore, she's your
opposite!"

"In color, at least!" laughingly responded Harry, for the
woman was as black as the ace of spades.

Bill in a moment, captured two more of the unwilling dam-
sels and then turned to the music.

"Tune up, and let us have it hot and lively!   Ladies square
yourselves—curchy to your partners, and then go it heel and
toe-nail!   Ellslerize yourselves!"

The music struck up and the dance commenced.   It was a
rich sight, the reader may fancy, to see the elegantly dressed
Whitmore and Livingston handing around their dirty, dusty
partners, *chassez*-ing and promenading, using the same mincing
steps and fancy figures which are most in vogue in the fashionable *assemblees*.

Bill however went in for a little heavier work, and "broke
down" like a real plantation boy in all kinds of double-shuffles
and juba steps till he made the very house shake.

His friend Ned Shorter, who, as if in contradistinction to his
name, was a head *higher* than any man in the room, and a
splendidly, elegantly-formed fellow at that, went it also, with
a "vindictive looseness," if we may be permitted to quote the
language of a city poet.

At last the dance was through, and Bill cried to his companions—

"Trot your gals up to the bar, boys! It's the fashion here, and we're bound to keep up the style, of course!"

The party of eight went to the bar, and Pete this time handed out the black bottle, for he saw that Bill's hand was in his pocket, and there was a chance for pay.

The liquor was drank, and then Bill threw down a dollar on the counter, ordering at the same time liquor to be mixed for the two at the door.

After this was done, the four at the bar joined the two at the door, and a consultation took place among them, the question being what next to do in the way of raising fun.

"We must have a fight!" said Butcher Bill.

"What shall it be?" asked Mr. Shorter,—"a genteel knock down, or a knock down and drag out?"

"A genteel one at first!" replied Bill, "and then for a general muss to close up with."

"Well, go ahead. Shall you call it up, or I?"

"Me *of* course!" responded Bill, "I'm more used to niggers than you are!"

As he said this, he stepped out into the middle of the room and cried in a careless, free and easy tone:

"I've come here to whip a nigger. Is there any one here that would like to take a quiet, genteel buff with me—fair play *and* no gouging?"

Not one of the negroes stirred, but some of them looked rather wolfish. The sailors now came in from Andy's room, and a circle began to be formed, for every one saw that a fight was inevitable.

Old Pete came out from behind his bar, and walking up to Bill, begged in the most imploring terms.

"Now do, Massa Bill, go 'way and not raise a muss! I'll give you ten dollar to go. You'll ruin all de respectable ob my 'stablishment!"

"Get out of the way old mutton-head, or I'll put you to sleep for a little while, and give you the nose bleed worse than I did that door-keeper of yours who wanted to charge gentlemen for admittance. Look at him in the corner and see how you'd like his fix!"

Williams saw that there was no use in reasoning with such a character, and he went back to his bar to put the tumblers and decanters out of reach in case that a general fight should occur.

Once more Butcher Bill defied any one of the negroes to fight him. None of them seemed desirous of being whipped by him. But he was not to be kept out of his fun in this way. He walked up to a herculean negro, a fellow who stood full six feet high, and was built very heavily.

"Your name is Zack Reed, and you're a states-prison bird!" said he, as he looked the fellow in the face.

"Well, dat isn't no business o' yourn!" said the negro gruffly.

"The devil it aint. You're as crooked-legged as a kangaroo!" and as he said this the bully kicked the negro heavily on the shin.

He almost turned pale with anger and pain, but he did not seem to desire the courted combat, for he said:

"Jist you go 'way from me white man! I isn't adoin o' nuthin to you, and I don't want to!"

"You're a coward, you don't dare to fight!" replied the bully.

"I doesn't want to fight. If I did I'd chaw you up and spit you out again afore you knowed whar you was, whiteman. Now jist keep away, and luff dis ere child be!"

Bill was determined now to have a fight at any rate, so he took a chew of tobacco from his mouth, and threw directly at one of the negro's eyes. He did not miss his aim, and the next moment, Zack, howling with the pain produced by the tobacco juice, rushed in upon him.

Bill met him with a blow between the eyes which would have felled an ox, but it did not move the negro, though it sounded like a blow from a hammer on a log of wood. Zack closed with him in a minute—the next second both of them fell to the floor. They were closely clenched; blows and curses came from both, yet no one interfered. This continued for about a minute, when the white man got on top of the other, and placing his knees on the negro's arms, so disabled him, that he had time to plant four or five terrible blows directly in the eyes and mouth of the latter.

This settled him, for each blow was like that given from a slege hammer, and bones were heard to crack and crush as he struck. The negro could stand no more, and he now cried enough.

Bill let him get up, and the poor fellow staggered off to the back room to wash away the blood.

"Now is the time for fun !" shouted Bill, as he arose.—" Let it be knock down and drag-out boys !"

As he said this, he commenced knocking down every one in his reach. Of course the negroes all rushed on him, but in a second Ned Shorter's tall form was seen, and at each blow he gave, a darkie *laid down*. Bill Lord and Dutch Charley, too were at work, and while they did things up scientifically, Gus. and Harry went to the same business, *en amateur*.

But this did not last long—the lights were put out, and when Bill gave the word his whole party walked out, striking down and trampling over every negro whom they met or felt as they made their way to the door. And thus at nearly four o'clock in the morning, ended ONE OF PETE WILLIAMS' BALLS.

CHAPTER XIII.

In a neatly furnished room, in a quiet boarding-house, up in the aristocratic part of the city, sat a gentleman of your acquaintance, reader. Dressed in a neat morning gown, embroidered slippers on his feet, a Turkish smoking cap on his head, a cigar in his hand, he looks like one of those who know how, if they have a chance, to take the world easy.

He seemed to be about half asleep, and as his feet were upon a table, and his head laid well back in an easy chair, it seemed very probable that it would not take him long to be entirely so.

But destiny disappointed this, for a rap was heard at his door, and as he sprang to his feet, he said:

"Come in."

The door half opened, and a very red-headed servant, with an exceedingly fresh brogue, said:

"There's a jintleman below stairs, yer Lordship's honor, as sez he wants to see yez!"

"Ver well—tell zat I shall ave ze pleasure of—no, not zat. You go and ask him what his name is!"

"Sure, yer lordship, but it's on this bit o' paste-board, he tould me!" and the servant put a whole body of very long but narrow dimensions into the room, and handed a card.

The gentleman looked at it a moment, then said:

"Ah, ha! Yes, zis is my ver goot frent, Messieur Carlton. Tell him to make himself up ze stair—zat I shall be ver glad for to see him."

Then, while the servant was gone upon this errand, the gentleman hastily stepped to the pier glass, and arranged his fine dark hair, and superb moustache.

The next momentt his door opened, and in walked Mr. Henry Carlton. He paused at the threshold, having shut the door behind him, and for a moment gazed steadfastly upon our friend with the moustache.

The latter seemed to enjoy his look of surprise very much, for he acknowledged it by his smile, but he did not speak.

Carlton did, however.

"By Jupiter!" he cried, "it is impossible! That is not you, Tobin?"

"If it is not me, Messieur Carlton, I should ver much like to know who it is!"

"Well, I never saw such a transformation in all my life. You will succeed to a T."

"Ah, sare, you flattare me; but about ze announce*mont*, eh!"

"It is all right," and Carlton took a paper from his pocket, from which he read this paragraph.

"We have heard from an undoubtedly correct source, that a very distinguished stranger from France is travelling *incog.* in this country, and that he is at present sojourning in this city, taking observations of our society and manners. He is said to be a nobleman, an officer of high rank in the army of his country, and a gentleman of remarkable accomplishments. We hope that he will not hide himself from the civilities and attentions which our first families are ever ready and anxious to pay to men of his rank."

"How do you like that," asked Carlton, when he had finished reading the article.

"I like it ver much, particular*lee* zat part which 'ave say I ave ze ver remarkable accomplish*mont!* I sink I shall prove zat by an bye, eh!" replied Captain Tobin, twirling his false moustache with a graceful air.

"Well, you shall have the chance. I know two or three families to whom I can get you introductions, and we'll soon work up a game for them. I have sent marked papers to them, and you'll find plenty of invitations as soon as you are known to be COUNT DELAMERE, Captain in the army of France.

"Well, I shall do zem ze honare of my companie, an I sink I shall make some ver gran speculatione!"

"Of course you will. Your disguise is very perfect. All that we need in our whole party is concentration, unity and industry, to make immense fortunes. There never was a better coalition in the world than our gang forms, if we only work together."

"Zat is ver true, Messieur, ver true!"

"Well, I'll not stay any longer—I'll call in occasionally to see how the cards work with you. Good morning."

"Good morning, sare—bon voyage! Adieu!" and the polite pickpocket, now the COUNT DELAMERE, bowed out his visitor.

The reader may be curious to know the red-headed servant found out the new rank of the illustrious boarder, and we will explain.

When Tobin was driven to the door of this boarding house, where he had learned before, they had " vacant rooms for *genteel* boarders,"—none others of course are ever advertised for—he inquired of the lady who kept it, if she could accommodate a gentleman who wished to live very privately with fine rooms. He was very willing to *pay* handsomely.

The lady was of course struck with his *distingue*, foreign air, she admired his manners and moustache, and soon showed him rooms which he said were very suitable. She did not tell him that she turned out a very interesting young lady—a music-teacher and preceptress in drawing, who had occupied that parlor and bed-room for several months—for she did this in a few minutes, while she left him in a lower parlor. The poor girl had not payed her board for about two weeks, having been too sick to receive her scholars, but the landlady thought the next story back bed-room was comfortable enough for the young lady ; though there was no fire-place in it.

Mr. Tobin therefore secured the rooms, and the talkative landlady managed with great tact to get a knowledge of his rank and name, promising, of course, inviolable secrecy, which promise she kept just as long as it took her to get into the vicinity of one who would help her to keep it.

But off we must go to another scene which, when it developes itself, will be found connected with the first part of this chapter.

The house where this scene is laid is not a mile from **Astor Place.** Within one of those large and elegant houses which front on ———— street; in the splendidly furnished sitting-room are four persons. Let me introduce you to Montague Fitz Lawrence and three members of his family, his wife and two sons. He has a daughter, but she is at the boarding-school. Mr. Fitz Lawrence is rich, *very* rich, for he has left off business, and now lives in style. His servants are all in livery—he keeps a fine carriage, and each of his sons drive a very fast team for themselves. They are educated—that is, educated for city-life. They know Pat Hisen and his set, are members of *the* club, where ere long we will see them. They can walk down Broadway and tell you the name of every woman (not *lady*) that they meet; they can play a fine game of billiards, smoke, drink and swear quite *elegantly*, or, as I once heard a romantic young lady say, " *divinely.*"

Mr. Fitz Lawrence had always been known as "Monty Lawrence," until he became wealthy, when a man versed in heraldry suddenly discovered through a pair of golden spectacles, that Monty meant Montague, and that Fitz certainly belonged to the original name. Moreover this good friend found out that a coat of arms belonged to them, one with sabres, Turks heads, and dragons on it. This of course was engraved on the "family plate," and also placed on their coach panel.

Mr. Fitz Lawrence was a very aristocratic man in all his feelings and predilections, and of course this made him gain many enemies, who were fond of talking about him. These often said that he used to keep a grog shop in the very centre of the "Points," but of course this was a foul slander, for he was a *gentleman.* And in his helpmate he had a very excellent specimen of aristocratic dignity.

Mrs. Fitz Lawrence was built much on the same principle as a dutch galliot; and had a face which we cannot easily describe, so the reader will please take our artist's delineation of the same.

One of the young men was named Alfred Eustace Fitzroy; the other was Gustavus Alexander Manvers Fitz Lawrence.

At the moment when we introduced this party to our readers, the old gentleman was reading the morning paper and had cast his eye upon the article alluding to the distinguished foreigner. He read it aloud, while his sons and especially his lady listened with breathless interest.

"I do wonder who it *can* be!" exclaimed Mrs. F. L. after her husband had concluded. "How I should like to give him a suwaree!"

"A what, mother?" asked Alfred Eustace, &c.

"Why a suwaree, too be sure, child! Dont you think I know what I mean?" and the lady tossed her head very indignantly at the insult which her son had given to her dignity.

"You mean a soiree, mother, I guess!" replied the youth.

"Well, I 'spose I do, but I will have my own way of calling things and it's not your business, nor nobody's, as long as I like it!" replied the lady, turning very red in the face.

"Well, I mean to find out where he lives—I know a man who knows every body that comes here!" cried Gustavus Alexander Manvers.

"Do, my good boy, do find him out. We'll show him what the aristocracy of America is! We'll make him feel that we know what good breeding is!" exclaimed the mother.

"I calculate we come of as good a stock as him—I wonder if he mightn't be related to our family. I must look at his coat of arms!" said the old gentleman, removing his spectacles and wiping them with the lining of his coat tail.

"Oh, I do wish that they had *rank* in this low country;

counts and countesses—lords and lordesses! There's no tellin' who's who, nor nothin', the way society is!" and as she said this Mrs. Fitz Lawrence's face assumed its exceedingly expressive sneer.

"It's a mortal fact—I never can get used to it!" added the old gentleman, and then he replaced his spectacles on his nose, and recommenced reading.

The young men arose and left the room—the mother did the same.

CHAPTER XIV.

It was cold, drizzly and dreary on the morning when Angelina and her mother left their room in Laight street, each carrying a bundle, on their way to their intended abode the Brewery.

It was scarcely dawn and very few persons were stirring in the streets—only such as necessity forced out. No one noticed Angelina and her mother, for they hurried along quietly, carrying their little all with them in those two bundles. Their newly presented furniture was left in the room for the disinterested Livingston to claim.

Down to the "Points" the two helpless females trudged, and when they got there, they found everything very still and quiet, for people who carouse and revel all night, and thieves who labor in the night, are apt to sleep late.

They paused before the Brewery, and as they looked up at the dirty walls of the immense building, Angelina sighed and said:

" This is the place, mother !"

" Well, child, it doesn't look so awful bad after all !"

" No, not on the outside, mother, but they say it is a dreadful place when you get in. But *he* won't follow us here !"

The mother was about to make some reply to her child, but was interrupted by a short, fat, very red-faced, vulgar-looking fellow who stood on the steps of a room which was used as a " grocery" in the front of the house.

" What ar you arter ? D'ye want a room, wimmen?" said he.

" Yes, sir," responded Angelina—" we are looking for a place to live !"

" Well, my clunk o' beauty, you've spotted the right place and run afoul of the right feller, if you've got the dust to pay your rent. I'm the agent of this ere 'stablishment, I am !"

As the fellow spoke his form and face fairly puffed out with the importance of his situation.

"We want a room, sir, and we are willing to pay for it," said the poor girl, timidly, shrinking from the rude gaze of the coarse, vulgar fellow.

"Well, you can get it—let me see—I've three left. Where'll you have it, up stairs or down?"

"We do not care, if it is only quiet!" replied Angelina.

"Not hard to please, eh? Come along, and look at 'em!" and as the man said this he led the way around to the entrance at the side of the house known to us in a former chapter, as murderer's alley.

He passed in and paused at a door about midway of the passage.

"There's a room on the second floor here, as is empty," said he—"and you can have it for fifty cents a week, payable in advance, invariably."

"Let us see it, sir, if you please," said Angelina, who seemed in this case to take the business all upon herself.

"Sartainly! Walk up ladies and suit yourselves. Our prices range from twenty-five cents up to one dollar!"

Angelina and her mother followed the man up a narrow pair of creaking stairs which were so thick with dirt that they seemed to walk upon sand, until they reached the second flight, where the man kicked open a door on his left hand.

It opened into a narrow stall, lighted dimly by one window, which had been smashed out of glass. There was a fire-place in it, but scarcely a sign that fire had ever been there. In one corner lay a small heap of stuff which once had been straw, but now it was as "fine cut" as Mrs. Miller's tobacco, and looked as if the mice had been resting in it for years.

No furniture at all was in sight.

The daughter gazed at it in silence, but the mother after one look, cried:

"How *can* we live here, child! It is dreadful, we can't stay here—we'll die!"

"Better *die* here, mother, than live in vice, though the dome of a palace sheltered us!"

"True child—very true.   But *can* we live here?"

"Yes, mother, wherever God pleases to send us.   We are his creatures—not our own!

"Well, wimmen, will you take the room?" asked the agent.

"Yes—we will take it, but we must have wood and food!" replied the girl.

"Well, lay down the dust—change, I mean, and then consider the room your own!"

The mother drew out her purse, which by the way, was made out of the toe of an old stocking, and handed him the fifty cents for the rent.

"All right," said he; "now, if you want fire-wood, or any thin' to eat, just come down and take it."

"Thank you, sir, we must have both fuel and provisions!" replied Angelina.

"Well, my gal, just come down and get what you want. I'll sarve you right, never fear—as long as you 'ave the money to pay for it.   My store is close underneath, where I was standin' when we first spotted each other."

"I'll come, sir.   We *need* many things," said Angelina, tearfully, for she thought of the good things which her mother had left behind her.

The man left the room, and Angelina followed him, with some change, to get a few necessary articles.

These he supplied her with, at a very low price—for things *must* be cheap here.   Then she returned to her mother, and the two tried to arrange their little room.   One of the large bundles which they had lugged down, contained their bed-clothing, and though they had been obliged to leave their cot-frame behind, by the help of some straw which Angelina bought of the agent, they managed to make a very comfortable bed-place.   A small fire was lighted in the little hearth-place, and   far as such a place *could* look cheerful, this did.   Angelina had worked with a gladness in fixing these things, which surprised her mother, for the poor young girl felt that her persecutor would not dream of following here, and this one great danger so absorbed her mind, that she feared or thought of no other—though many and terrible ones were now around her.   Of these she had no knowledge, therefore, was as secure in her own mind, as if they were not.

"We must have work now, mother!" said Angelina, "we shall have to work very hard now, for this room will be very cold without fire."

"Yes, child—but we've some money left; take to-day, at least, for rest."

"I will until to-night, mother, for I fear to go out in the day-light, lest I should meet *him*. But when night comes, I shall go down to the store and get more work."

The mother was interrupted in her reply, by a heavy knock on the door.

The daughter trembled from head to foot.

"Oh, God, it may be *he!* if it is, do not let him in, dear mother —save me as you love your child!"

A coarse female voice outside, soon dispelled this fear of the poor girl, for it cried:

"Is any body lives here, sure?"

"Go open the room door, mother—it is some poor Irish wo-man!" said Angelina, ceasing now to tremble, but still standing in the farthest corner of the room.

The mother unfastened the door, which was closed by a hasp and staple on the inside, and as she did so, a large, red-faced, filthy-looking woman entered. Her dirty neck, and great flabby bosom was almost entirely uncovered—her dress was ragged, and so scanty in its skirt that she exposed large swollen legs and ankles, stockingless at that, and full of those festering, disgusting blotches, called rum-sores. A pair of old cast-off men's shoes were on her feet, but the toes looked for daylight through numerous openings. She had nothing on her head save a very scanty quantity of grizzly, uncombed hair.

As she came in, she nodded her head, and cried:

"The agint tould me that some new neighbors had come, and I've come to say, how d'ye, and visit yez. Me name is *Missis* Haggerty, sure, and it's meself that's a lady born and bred, only it's a little poor I've been lately!"

The widow and Angelina looked at the strange woman, but

neither of them spoke; between their fear and disgust, they were speechless.

But Missis Haggerty was not to be put off in her visits. She walked into the room, and with her red and swollen eyes, looking Angelina rudely in the face, said:

"An' it's a purty face yez have got, Miss; I'll be bound that ye've lots o' lovers!"

"No—I never have any," replied the poor girl, feeling that she *must* speak and not offend the strange visitor.

"Niver have ony? Och, an' it's yerself that's a bloody fool, then, wid yer purty looks. Yez could make lots o' money."

The girl shuddered, but did not reply. The woman continued:

"Is it a bit o' baccy ye'd be after givin' me to fill my pipe wid?"

"We have no tobacco; we never smoke!" replied the widow, gathering a little more courage.

"Niver smoke? Why it's yerselves then as don't know what a blissed life is. You've a mere drap o' gin for a poor sick crater, tho'?"

"No, we never drink, either!"

"Not drink gin, sure?" exclaimed the woman, and her face seemed to try to express both astonishment and contempt. Why, I thought yez wor Christian wimmen an' ye're no better than haythens! May yez have a saxpence about yez, that ye'd lind to a poor woman as is a lady born, for wid it I can have a drink an' smoke!"

"I've no change less than a shilling," replied the widow.

"Then give me the shillin' jist, an' meself 'll git it changed for yez!"

The mother took out her little stock and picking out a shilling handed it to the woman, but she did not mark how the eyes of the sick woman glared at the little handful of change which was left, even as a beast looking upon its prey.

But she took only the shilling, as she did so, saying:

"It's meself that 'll niver forget yez. I live yer nex door neighbor, an' it's often I'll come an' see yez. I'll not let yez be lonesome, for yez ar Christian folks, for all yez don't drink or smoke. I'll do that same for ye, whiniver I can raise the dust!"

After she said this, the woman hurried away to get her gin and tobacco, while the widow closed the door again.

"I knew it would be horrible—but yet this is better than *his* persecution!" murmured poor Angelina, as she sank down upon their little pallet of straw, to which the mother also came.

"Let us try and sleep, mother, we will work to-night after I come home from the store!" said Angelina.

The mother only replied by bursting into tears, and putting her arms around her child's neck.

"Don't weep, mother. It is wrong to cry. Do you not remember my song, never despair? The cloud is always the darkest where the bright lightning is about to break forth. God cares for us—let us trust to Him!"

"We will, my angel child, we will, but this place is horrible!"

"Hope, faith, and love, will make the darkest place bright, mother. Now *do* stop crying, and let us sleep in each other's arms, as we so often have done!"

"But that dreadful woman may come back."

"The door is fastened, mother."

"So it is, child. I had forgotten that."

The mother now ceased to weep, and interlocked in each other's arms, they went to sleep.

15

CHAPTER XV.

IT was but a few moments after the night had set in, in fact it was yet twilight. Tremblingly as she crept down the narrow stairs and out through the filthy, horrible-smelling alley, poor Angelina started for the store of her employers to get work. Once out in the street, she ran as fast as her feeble limbs would carry her, for now the streets were full of men and women, and strange sights and stranger sounds met her ear as she hurried along.

But soon she was in Centre street, clear of the Points, and now she had to pause to regain her breath. After doing so, she walked up toward the Park more slowly, avoiding to raise her head, and drawing her thick hood close around it.

When she arrived at the head of Beekman street, she turned off to cross into Nassau street, down which her way led to her employer's store, but as she stopped to wait for an omnibus to pass, the light of the lamp above her shone full upon her and one of a party of young men who were on the other side saw it.

"By thunder, there she is! On her trail once more and curse me if I leave it!" shouted the young man, and as he hurried across the street, his companions shouted:

"Go it Gus.! The devil catch the hindmost!"

Poor Angelina heard that voice, and with a wild shriek turned and rushed through the open gate into the park. On—on she fled, but she heard his step close behind her. Her limbs trembled under her—her breath grew short. She saw a female dress before her, and rushing up to its wearer, while she clasped the dress, and fell to the earth, shrieked:

"Oh, save me—save me from him!"

"What's the matter, my little chick?" cried the gruff voice of one who before had spoken to her, and the terrified girl recognized in it, her former protector, Big Lize.

"Oh, save me once more! Look, *he* comes!" and as the young girl spoke she pointed to Livingston, who was already close upon them.

Drawing back the poor girl with her left hand, as the villain came within her reach, Lize planted a blow between his eyes which would have knocked down an ox. It left him perfectly senseless.

The woman now took the sewing-girl by the hand, and led her out into Broadway.

When she got under a lamp, she paused and looked Angelina in the face. As she did so, the memory of the other scene came up in a moment.

"Why, is it you?" How comes it, that when you are in trouble, I'm always near?"

"I know not, but Heaven will bless you as I do, for saving me from him!"

"Blessings! blessings!" murmured Lize—"Oh, gal, you are innocent yet, keep so—keep *so!*" and her eyes filled with tears, as she bent over the sewing-girl, and kissed her.

As she did so, Angelina returned her kiss fervently, and while with one arm, she clasped her neck in gratitude, with the other hand, she tried to wipe away the tears which streamed down the cheeks of the woman. Suddenly the eye of the latter glanced upon the ring which was on the girl's finger. She looked at it closely, then almost screamed:

"For the love of God, tell me where you got that ring!"

"It was my father's!" replied Angelina.

Your *father's?* Oh, God! *girl, who are you?*"

"Who am I? What is the matter,—why do you clench my hand so hard? You hurt me! Why do you stare at me so wildly?"

"Girl—if you love your God, answer me one question! What is your family name?"

"My father's name was Lindsay—James Lindsay!"

"Oh, God, is it so! Are you yet pure—yet free from that damning, fearful taint which is sinking me into hell?"

"I don't know what you mean. I never have done wrong— *I never will?*"

" Thank God ! thank God ! If I am miserable, you yet shall be happy ! I am—but no, I will not tell you now.   Another time, and I will !"

END OF PART SECOND.